A CLOSER WALK

A Couple's Inspiring

True Story about

Faith after Tragedy

Sharon Faber

A CLOSER WALK
Copyright © 2018 by Sharon Faber

Printed in Canada

ISBN: 978-1-4866-1655-8

Word Alive Press
119 De Baets Street, Winnipeg, MB R2J 3R9
www.wordalivepress.ca

Cataloguing in Publication may be obtained through Library and Archives Canada

I dedicate this book to Jesus Christ, who guided me through the writing process and has held my hand every step of the way. It is also dedicated to every dear person who has supported our family over the years by praying for us—I am eternally grateful.

A special thank you is extended to Al and Denise Tupper for their unforgettable support, and to Sheryl Martin for encouraging me to share my story.

CONTENTS

INTRODUCTION

Recently I've been struggling with death—specifically the death of my husband, Ken. Fears of him leaving me tormented me constantly, hindering my peace of mind. Each day during our morning farewell, I'd wonder if this would be our last goodbye, which ensured I waved one last time—just in case. When the phone rang at an unusual time, I'd wonder if the dreaded call had come. I would wake up in the night to find myself composing his eulogy in my mind. Over and over I found myself pondering and wondering what my life would be like without him. But I also knew these fears were futile, as no one knows the number of days left until we breathe our last—only the Lord who created us.

One morning in the fall of 2014, I reached my limit. I couldn't go on like this any longer, couldn't continue living with this dread, this fear, as it tainted every part of my life. Crying out to God for help, He heard my cry, answered my prayer, and removed my fears. But He also asked me to set aside one year to write down our story, to tell what God has done for me and my family. I've never shared my memoirs before, never sat down and told the story from beginning to end, but the Lord has helped me take this one step at a time. My prayer is that, by the end of the last page, He will have told our story.

Twenty years. I've been waiting twenty years to tell our story. Where do I begin?

Chapter One

THE UNEXPECTED

S tanding in a lonely phone booth, I heard the news. Still holding the phone's receiver in my hand, I turned my head to look at the peaceful view of our lake, trees heavy with their summer coat of leaves, unchanging granite rocks and islands as familiar to me as my own hand, our happy cottage just out of sight around the bend of the shoreline, but everything slightly distorted by the smudgy plastic window of the phone booth. In the distance I heard the drone of a motorboat and the high whine of buzzing cicadas, but it was the sound of the dial-tone that caught my attention and, in slow motion, I replaced the heavy black receiver, realizing that my life had changed, never to be the same again.

Only yesterday we had said our goodbyes. I was going away, taking our young boys to my parents' cottage for a few days. His goodbye bear hug was the highlight of my day. I remembered the last time I saw him. He stood at the back door of our house wearing his worn work boots, laces untied and trailing, battered lunchbox gripped in one hand with the other hand resting gently on the door handle, impatient to start his day but standing still, looking at me with his clear blue eyes and slight smile. This is the image I have carried of him in my mind for many years. I didn't know this would be the last time I'd see him standing just like this.

When you least expect it, life will eventually trip you up. You'll fall. Hard. You thought the world was rosy and lovely, but what happens when it isn't? When from complete darkness you cry, "Where is the light?" Where is hope when the pit of pain you're in is deeper than your worst nightmare? Who do you turn to when the world turns against you? What do you do when life stops being magical?

On my shelf I have a dog-eared, handwritten journal documenting the unforgettable event my family faced in 1993. The time has come to take it out, dust it off, and crack it open. This tale has changed my life—and the time has come to share it.

———

The morning of Wednesday, August 11, 1993 held the promise of becoming a perfect day at my parents' cottage. My two boys, four-year-old James and two-year-old John, were with me along with my closest friend, Lauralynn Mercer, and her two sons who were the same ages as mine. My husband, Ken, was in the stifling heat of the city, working.

Everyone was out enjoying the sunshine as it shone down onto the hot wooden dock while a faint breeze rippled the lake water, causing it to flash like handfuls of flung diamonds. The boys' small, suntanned bodies glistened as they played in the warm lake, strapped into orange life jackets with brilliantly coloured wet swim shorts clinging to their chubby legs. The sweet smell of sunscreen hung in the air and enhanced the lazy feeling creeping over us. Lauralynn and I sprawled out in lounge chairs, she reading an informative book about nutrition with me engrossed in the timeless drama of *Pride and Prejudice*.

The sound of my neighbour's voice surprised me.

"Hello, Sharon."

I awkwardly hastened to sit up, as I hadn't heard him approach. He had dropped by to relay a message from my mom to call her. We didn't have a telephone at the cottage and I didn't carry a cell phone. My neighbour left as suddenly as he'd appeared and I knew something serious—something bad—had happened. I was reluctant to leave the dock's sheltered cocoon of safety to discover what awful news awaited me.

Opening the car door, pent-up heat rushed out and threatened to suffocate me. I slid onto the hot seat to drive to the local phone booth. It sat by itself—isolated—on the side of the lake's shore road. I parked the car, fumbled for a quarter in my purse, and drew in a large breath to fortify myself, reluctant to dial the number.

Mom told me that Ken had been hurt at work and I should return home. It seemed unreal. Hurt at work? Ken in trouble—alone and hurting?

I then called my sister, Linda, for more details. I sensed she was upset by her tense voice. Ken had been injured and airlifted to a hospital in Toronto. We made arrangements for me and the kids to drive to her house. Then her husband, Alex, would take us downtown.

The call disconnected, but I still held the receiver. Watching my hand slowly hang it up, I felt detached. This couldn't really be happening. It must be a mistake. Airlifted! The realization washed over me that Ken was in trouble, but I never imagined how critical the situation was or the extent of how our lives would change.

Back at the cottage, my mind wouldn't work. I'd closed up the cottage dozens of times, but this time I had trouble remembering what to do next. Our suitcases had to be packed, the fridge emptied, garbage gathered, windows closed, the power turned off, and the door locked behind us.

While I was busy with this, Lauralynn prepared peanut butter sandwiches for the four boys to eat on the two-hour drive back to Brampton where we all lived. I was thankful Lauralynn was with me so I didn't have to drive by myself.

Our serious attitude rubbed off on the kids, because they ate their sandwiches quietly, their usual playful banter stilled. The ride was uneventful. Part of me didn't want it to end, so I could stay in the safe bubble called Ignorance.

Arriving at Linda's house, the first part of the journey over, I was surprised to see a crowd of people waiting for me. Linda had called a friend to babysit her children and our friends, the Rogers, to take care of mine, even making arrangements for an overnight stay. Outside in the sunshine, I knelt down on the hard driveway to hug James and John goodbye, remembering yesterday's hug Ken and I had shared together.

As we drove away, I waved to them and my fake, plastic-like smile wavered. My face slowly crumpled and I fumbled in my purse for a Kleenex, unable to stop the trickling tears. This was the first time I cried.

Several minutes passed before I succeeded in regaining my composure. From where I sat in the back seat behind Linda, I had a clear view of the gas gauge. The red needle pointed to empty, even beyond empty, and the calm I'd worked to achieve started to drain away, like the fuel slowly draining out of the tank. Alex, who was married to my sister and was also Ken's brother, assured me not to worry; there was plenty of gas left. Here I was, stressed out, in the middle of a crisis, and I found myself struggling with a familiar family trait—running the car on empty. The car was running on fumes, by the look of the gauge, but I decided to take Alex's suggestion and not let it worry me. I had more important thoughts to occupy my mind.

We were headed to Toronto Western Hospital in downtown Toronto.

Rob Arrives

I was the first one to arrive at the hospital. At an appointment not far away, I received a call that Ken, my older brother, had been seriously injured at a construction site. From the gut-wrenching, sinking feeling I had in the pit of my stomach, I sensed things were bad—very bad.

With shaking hands I reached for my map book, riffling through the pages to navigate the quickest route to the hospital. Ken was my older brother by only eighteen months. We'd done everything together since we'd been little squirts—our whole lives were intertwined, as close as two brothers could be. In times of crisis, we were always ready to bail out the other and face the tough times side by side. I wondered what scrape he had fallen into this time.

After parking, I followed the signs to the Emergency Department. My premonition proved correct when I learned Ken was in the Trauma Unit. Seconds after asking for him, two young doctors with crossed arms stood in front of me, trying to block my way. They said I couldn't see Ken, that they weren't allowing visitors yet. I squared my shoulders and, from my six-foot-three-inch height, with hands on my hips, glared down at them. No one was going to stand between me and Ken, to prevent me from reassuring him that I was close by. They didn't resist when

I stepped between them, brushed past, and continued walking down the busy hallway.

Outside the Trauma Unit, I paused for a second to compose myself, took a deep breath, and stepped inside.

Ken was a mess. There was blood everywhere—smeared, red and sticky, on the side of his face and shoulder. A clean white brace had been tightly fastened around his tanned neck and he was slipping in and out of consciousness. I bent down close to him, telling him I was there, that he wasn't alone, and squeezed his hand. As I left, a nurse said that Ken was scheduled for a CT scan and pointed me towards the waiting room.

Ken and I were united again, but this time fighting a battle between life and death, a battle that would change both our lives.

Judging by everything I had heard so far, and by the tight knot I felt deep within me, I doubted Ken's survival. The outcome, I knew, looked bleak and a hopeless darkness settled over me.

I found the waiting room, fit my tall frame into an uncomfortable vinyl chair, and started my long vigil—waiting.

Ken Heads to Work

That morning, I woke up to sunshine streaming through my window and stretched my legs under the blanket, relishing having the bed to myself. My wife, Sharon, and our two young sons were at the lake enjoying the hot summer weather.

I'll never forget the day she caught my eye, stepped into my life, and stole my heart. Her dark shoulder-length hair and brown eyes complemented my fair colouring. She approached life with a no-nonsense attitude but was also quick with a sparkling smile that lit up her face. Her dry sense of humour helped her see the funny side of almost anything, even when things went wrong. I'm the easy-going type and I help Sharon to relax and enjoy life—not take it too seriously. She's good for me, though. I'd be lost without her as she helps me stay focused.

Throwing back the blanket, I jumped out of bed, eager to start the day.

The house was unnaturally quiet and not quite as orderly as Sharon had left it. On the kitchen table sat a disassembled hydraulic motor with greasy parts radiating out around it. I thought I should probably clear the mess away before she returned home, but if I didn't have time, she'd get over it. This is a favourite saying of mine: "You'll get over it." Why get upset over things that don't really matter?

I grabbed some yogurt and a couple of apples for my lunch, locked the door, jumped into my old pickup truck, the door groaning in protest as I slammed it shut, and adjusted the radio to a local news station. The announcer reported that today would be blisteringly hot, so I rolled down my window and headed to King City, north of Toronto.

Stepping out of the truck, the heat brought beads of sweat out on my forehead. I reached into the truck for my baseball cap; not finding it, I put my white hardhat on instead. I strapped on my tool belt and strode through the site carrying my longest ladder, because the glass solarium my construction company was working on was on the second floor. It only needed a few finishing touches to complete.

When the other workers noticed my white hardhat, which normally indicated a supervisor, they thought I was the head site supervisor and scurried to don their hardhats to comply with safety regulations.

Up on the roof, I checked over the intricate skylights and fancy glasswork, calculating that there was only an hour of work left to do. The hour passed quickly. Still standing on my ladder, I was impressed by the quality of my crew's workmanship.

Beautiful job, done well, I thought to myself.

This moment marked the exact second everything changed.

Confused, I suddenly couldn't figure out where I was. My face was pressed against the unyielding concrete of the sidewalk. Still wearing my hardhat, I watched as a pool of blood slowly grew before my eyes.

What had happened? My body felt battered from head to toe like a farm tractor had mangled me, leaving every bone broken. I saw a pair of work boots standing nearby and mumbled, "Where am I?"

The work boots turned towards me and said, "King City at Jane and King Road."

Realization crept over me. I had fallen from the roof, twenty feet above. My receding puzzlement was replaced by overwhelming, searing pain, causing me to feel faint and then lose consciousness.

The paramedics stood beside me, their shadows protecting me from the glare of the sun. They said I'd have to wait a little longer for the helicopter to arrive as I was too badly injured to be transported by their nearby ambulance. Judging by the way I felt, I agreed and was relieved to hear the throbbing sound of the approaching chopper.

The paramedics tenderly moved me to a hard stretcher board and fastened the straps as tight as they could. To carry me to the waiting helicopter, they had to walk through soft sand; the movement of the stretcher with each sinking step brought unbelievable, excruciating pain. I clamped my teeth together and tried not to cry out in agony.

This movement didn't compare to the violent vibration the helicopter made during liftoff, though, and an even greater surge of intense pain caused everything to go black. I lost consciousness again.

Unfamiliar sounds surrounded me. I wasn't wearing my T-shirt, but instead wore a thin green gown. I was in the hospital. I asked a nurse where my clothes and work boots were only to hear they'd been cut off. That upset me—I liked those jeans and the shirt had been a thrift store special!

Clutching a clipboard, the nurse began asking the usual routine questions. She was checking to ensure I didn't have any medical conditions they should know about and that I was aware of my surroundings. I was determined to pass her test.

I was doing fine until she asked me where I was. Anxious that I'd failed her questionnaire, I had to admit I didn't know to which hospital I'd been taken. She told me I was at Toronto Western Hospital, then continued with her endless list of questions. Do you have any allergies? Any history of heart problems? Any respiratory issues? Any problems with your vision? I answered no to each question.

"Any problems with your hearing?" she asked.

"Pardon?" I asked innocently.

She repeated, a little louder, "Have you had any problems with your hearing?"

I again answered, "Pardon?"

She couldn't stop the laugh that bubbled up and shook her head when she realized I'd been joking with her.

Each time I regained consciousness, someone was asking a barrage of questions. Was I able to move my toe? Could I make a fist? Did this pinprick hurt? With a sense of relief, I felt consciousness slowly fade away.

A familiar voice said my name and I opened my eyes to see my brother, Rob, bending over me. In my peripheral vision, I noticed that he held my hand but it felt strangely numb, not like it should have.

Rob assured me that if I needed him, he'd be just outside the door. Before slipping into oblivion again, I wondered how he had managed to arrive so quickly.

From far away, deep inside my head, I heard the click of metal lightly tapping against metal. Each unfamiliar tap coincided with an increase of pain in my skull. I was now awake, my eyes wide open. A smock-clad stranger holding a wrench tightened a screw just inches above my eyes. Again the screw was tightened, increasing the pressure and pain.

"Hey!" I yelled. "You're going to crush my skull!"

The man stopped, explaining to me that this had to be done and he would soon be finished. He was screwing on a black metal frame called a halo. It encircled my head and had four pins which poked into my skull to immobilize my neck. At the end of each pin was a screw he had to tighten with a wrench. He said he'd be done in ten minutes and then the pain would stop.

When he finished, ten minutes later, I was relieved to find he'd been right. There was no longer any discomfort in my skull, but the halo failed to diminish the nightmarish, throbbing pain in the rest of my body.

Chapter Two

IDYLLIC BEGINNINGS

My dad, Alan Glendenning, worked in the printing industry as a lithographer and stayed with the same company for most of his career. He was a conservative man who worked hard, rarely taking unnecessary chances. I learned from him how to be faithful, even when it isn't easy. He married the love of his life, Ann, a flamboyant and artistic extrovert. My mom complemented Dad's staid demeanour with her live-life-to-the-full attitude, never allowing a dull moment to develop. Christ was the centre of their lives and their home.

I was their firstborn, a dark-haired girl named Sharon. Twenty-six months later, my sister, Linda, joined the family. Early in Alan and Ann's marriage, they bought a house in Brampton, put down long roots, and stayed until their retirement. Attending a local church, my dad volunteered as an usher for decades and my mom taught Sunday school, organizing Bible verse memorization contests for her class. As a family, we faithfully attended both the morning and evening Sunday services and the midweek Bible study.

When I was seven years old, my parents purchased a piece of land just large enough to build a cottage on, along the shore of a narrow lake called T-Lake. Dad built our cottage during summer vacations. Each Friday evening we piled into the car, which usually had lumber tied to the roof rack, and journeyed north. We started in May and made the trek until September or October, depending on the weather. One reason my parents chose T-Lake was that Dad's brother had a cottage across the lake. Another reason was the close proximity of an interdenominational chapel. Even though we went away each weekend, we still attended church.

Friends and cousins were always welcome and we hosted family reunions with regularity. We spent countless hours learning to swim in the warm water, floating on patched air mattresses with our toes in the lake, leaping off our cousin's diving board, and water skiing behind our old Starcraft boat with its white vinyl top and fifty-horsepower Evinrude outboard motor.

Linda and I were given an inflatable orange dinghy, just large enough to squeeze in the two of us. Because of the rocky shore, it constantly had a slow leak in need of patching. We paddled it on exploring expeditions around the lake, crawling out at convenient docks along the route to blow it back up with air after enough had leaked out to risk imminent sinking.

Mom let us escape to any adventure we'd dream up as long as we brought our life jackets along with us. It was cramped in the dinghy with two of us, a packed lunch, sandals, and our folded beach towels, so we'd tie the life jackets to a rope and float them along behind. On windy days we'd resurrect an old curtain, slide the handle ends of our paddles into the rod pocket and hem, hold up our homemade sail, and lean back to catch the wind. We'd skim over the water and be down the lake in a flash!

Our orange dinghy was a common sight to our neighbours, and it entertained us for endless hours.

We spent our summers flopped on sun-warmed rocks listening to water lapping gently on the shore, picking blueberries with one hand while swatting deer flies away with the other, exploring rocky islands that humped out of the water like turtle shells, investigating gurgling streams, rubbing Noxzema on strap-marked sunburns, riding our creaking bikes up and down the rutted gravel lane, jumping off our raft while holding our noses, buying sticky penny candy at the local marina, and peering into murky water through our swim masks. We were young and carefree and loved every minute of it. Cold water, bumps and bruises, insect bites, and rain didn't hold us back from setting out on our adventures. We were two tough little girls, but we weren't tomboys either. Mom had taught us to be young ladies.

One warm spring Sunday outside our church in Brampton, a red convertible with its top down roared up to the front door, then slowed to a creep as it passed the sidewalk. A frenzy of activity erupted as two young men burst out of the church, ripped off their shirts, and dove bare-chested into the open back seat. They were barely in, legs still hanging out, flapping shirts clutched in their hands like white flags, when the car squealed its tires and accelerated down the street, leaving behind an audience of parishioners, heads shaking in disbelief.

My dad was quite disgusted, thinking this inappropriate behaviour for a Sunday morning, and he called them a bunch of hoodlums. He couldn't have known that two of the four brothers, the eldest and the youngest, would become his cherished sons-in-law in a few short years.

———

Clarence and Joanne Faber, both born in the Netherlands, met, fell in love, and married in Brampton. Blessed with five fair-haired children, Ann, the only girl, was followed by Ken, Rob, Peter, and Alex. Their Christian home was bursting with laughter and fun-filled games.

Clarence, an entrepreneur, carved out his living building greenhouses, and later, solariums. With four sons, he had a ready-made work crew and they spent their summers, even when the boys were still quite young, building and working together. They were most comfortable adorned in work boots, tool belts strapped into place, and holding caulking guns. A strong work ethic was ingrained into them by their dad, but they always made time for laughter, friendly teasing, and joking together.

Being a physical family, they kept fit and made staying in shape a priority. They often encouraged each other with contests to discover who could do the most chin-ups, run the fastest, jump the farthest, or squeeze out the most sit-ups. Light-hearted brawls often broke out, perfect opportunities for them to demonstrate their affection for each other.

The two older boys, Ken and Rob, were inseparable and nicknamed Peter and Alex "the punks." Ken and Rob, only eighteen months apart, were competitive and their good-natured rivalry defined their relationship. In primary school, they joined the Chess Club and practiced playing against each other at home. After a few months, they became so evenly matched that whoever made the first move became the victor, each of them only one turn away from conquering the other.

High school introduced the intricacies of basketball and rugby into their relationship. Although Rob had the advantage in height, Ken made up for it in determination. In Rob's opinion, Ken wasn't the most talented athlete, but he was definitely the most determined. They carried basketballs with them everywhere—like extra appendages. Their high school buddies nicknamed Rob "Fabes" and Ken, because he was older, "Super Fabes." They treasured their high school years into adulthood, and to the chagrin of their children they frequently reminisced about their daredevil adventures, unbelievable antics, and great prowess in the field or on the court.

———

It was inevitable that Ken and I should meet, as we both attended the same church. I remember watching Ken's sister, Ann, with her long, wavy, strawberry-blond hair, walking into our young adult Sunday school class between Ken and Rob, their arms all linked together. The three of them looked striking, all with good looks and perfect smiles. Ken was a little over six feet, powerfully muscled with broad shoulders and lean hips. He had a deep, husky voice and a quick smile that showed off even white teeth. He had blond hair and tender blue eyes that revealed the vulnerability he tried to keep hidden.

One Sunday, I caught Ken's attention, but it's a mystery as to what caught Ken's attention first: me or the 1970 Chevrolet Malibu with a 307 V-8 engine I drove. It had a two-speed Powerglide transmission, a racing steering wheel, and a Thrush muffler which enhanced the throaty muscle car sound. Unfortunately, the driver's door didn't work very well. In fact, it didn't open at all. Crawling through the passenger side was the only way to access the driver's seat. This didn't seem to bother Ken, because while standing in the church lobby, with a crowd of chattering people around us, he asked me out on a date to go skiing with him. I hesitated for a few moments, not wanting to appear too eager, and then calmly accepted.

He drove his work-worn pickup truck to my house early on a sunny Saturday morning in January. While I gathered my ski gear, Ken waited in the living room. Dad sat in his favourite chair with a newspaper held up in front of his face, keeping a stony silence. He wasn't too pleased that "the hoodlum" was knocking on his door and calling on his daughter.

I had only skied downhill once before and Ken, an expert compared to my ability, never left my side or appeared impatient while waiting for me. When I happened to fall, Ken eagerly offered his assistance by gathering my dropped mitts and poles and gently brushing snow off my behind. By the end of the day, with some coaching tips from Ken, I had improved and skied better than when I'd first arrived. He ensured I kept warm, bought us lunch, and carried my heavy skis for me. He was the perfect gentleman.

Later in the day, he asked me my age and didn't believe my reply. I then asked him the same question and didn't believe him either. We decided to solve the dilemma by exchanging driver's licenses and were both relieved to discover our age difference was less than we had originally thought. Back then, I looked several years younger than eighteen and Ken looked about eight to ten years older than twenty.

That afternoon, after the slopes had closed for the day, Ken chose the longest route possible to drive me home. We sang along to the hits on the radio and he rhymed off every corny joke in his repertoire. I dutifully laughed after each one, not realizing they'd be repeated scores of times in the coming years.

He then asked me a direct question: "So, do you know how to cook?"

I thought this a strange inquiry for a first date, as it hinted at a seriousness I wasn't willing to explore. Why would he ask me that? Was he hoping I'd be cooking for him one day?

The question made me uncomfortable, so I gave an off-the-cuff answer. "If you can read a recipe, you can cook."

Then I changed the subject. Noticing my hesitation, Ken kept the conversation light-hearted for the remainder of the ride home.

We laughed and chatted, and I was pleased with the day. Because of the cooking question, I figured Ken was pleased, too, and my premonition proved correct when Ken, remembering my car door dilemma, invited me to his house the next weekend so he could repair it. Of course, I quickly accepted.

By our third or fourth date, I knew we had something special together. We didn't talk about it—we didn't have to—but we both knew we were meant for each other.

After dating several months, Ken and Rob flew to Austria for a long-anticipated ski trip, and the two weeks Ken was away dragged by at a snail's pace. A week after he left, I started to receive postcards which showed the picturesque views they were seeing firsthand with handwritten descriptions of what they were doing. This was my first exposure to Ken's poor spelling and indecipherable handwriting, but the words of love written from his heart more than compensated for his grammatical errors. Long after our reunion at the Toronto airport, the mailman continued to deliver postcards mailed weeks earlier. I still have them today, tucked among my treasures.

When I started dating Ken, he sported a bushy red beard. He liked to grow one each winter as he worked outside, even on the coldest days. He arrived one warm spring day clean-shaven and I failed to recognize him, wondering who this stranger was. When he said my name, recognition dawned. My heart flipped when I saw how handsome he was with his strong, square jaw with the cleft in his chin. He told me he had shaved it off because he was pleading not-guilty in court for a traffic ticket and wanted to appear as innocent as possible.

At the cottage, I taught Ken to water ski in icy cold water. Since I'd been water skiing every summer since I was ten years old, I was an accomplished skier. It bothered him to no end that I excelled at a sport he'd never tried before. After only a couple of unsuccessful attempts, he popped up on two skis and skied around the lake.

In the afternoon, he asked me to teach him to slalom ski. I tried to encourage him to practice longer on two skis before advancing to one ski, as he still looked shaky on the water and could barely cross the wake. My arguments were futile, as he continued to insist. Against my better judgment, I showed him how it was done. I couldn't believe my eyes when he succeeded right away—and did it so well! I've taught scores of people to water ski over the years, but Ken is the only one who learned in the morning and then slalomed in the afternoon.

He approached skiing differently than I did. I pushed myself to improve but did it gradually, which meant I rarely fell. Instead of commenting on how well Ken looked while he skied, we rated him on a scale of one to ten on how spectacular his wipeouts were. And there were plenty!

As Ken spent more time with my family, they grew to know him and witnessed how kind and gentle he was. Dad's earlier misgivings quickly vanished, replaced with genuine affection.

During this time, Rob was seeing a lovely girl, Carey, and the four of us enjoyed double dates together: fall country fairs, Chinese dinners, fun-filled amusement parks, snowmobiling over drifted snow, the odd game of golf, and vigorous hikes. Carey and I endured countless hours sitting side by side in cold, noisy arenas, huddled under heaters watching the guys play hockey—or at least pretending we were watching. I'm afraid we missed plenty of goals and referee calls that resulted in one of our men cooling his heels in the penalty box. Sometimes when the buzzer marked the end of the game, we weren't too sure which team had claimed victory, but we always jumped up and cheered when everyone around us did, occasionally cheering for the wrong team by accident.

———

I soon learned about The Rule. The Fabers had an important code they lived by, a line that was never crossed, a practice they still abide by today: no punching to the head—ever. This applies while play-fighting, even if rough-housing escalates into a real scrimmage.

One Sunday, Rob was chauffeuring us to the Fabers' home in Ken's old Mercedes after church. We were dressed in our Sunday best and enjoying the ride. The sun shone warmly through the windows, causing us to feel cosy while outside lay a glistening blanket of fresh snow. Peter sat in the front passenger seat, Ken and Alex took up the back seat, and I was squeezed between them, shoulder to shoulder.

Rob pulled into the Faber driveway and made the fatal decision to turn the car around, making it easier for us to get out. While completing his three-point turn, amid many conflicting directions from all male passengers about where to park, how to turn, how to slow down, and the distance behind us to the driveway edge, he still managed to get stuck in a snowbank. While the wheels spun ineffectively, Rob told Peter in a matter-of-fact voice to get out and push.

"Why should I have to push?" Peter grumbled. "You're the one who got us stuck."

Silence filled the car except for the softly playing radio. The rest of us felt lazy in the warm car. Nobody volunteered to assist.

Putting the car in park, Rob opened his door and stepped out. As he marched around the front of the car to the passenger side, all our heads turned in unison, wondering about his next move. He jerked open Peter's door, grabbed his collar, and yanked him out. While doing so, he accidentally knocked off Peter's glasses and bumped his head against the doorframe. Peter let out a yell of anger, pulled back his fist, and retaliated by punching Rob in the head. For a second or two, no one moved—he had broken the rule.

By the time the three of us crawled out of the back seat, it had escalated into an all-out fistfight with both of them yelling at each other.

"You punched me in the head!"

"You jerk, you hit *my* head on the car!"

Wearing their Sunday shoes, they lost their footing and fell in the snow together, arms thrashing and legs kicking.

From a safe distance, I asked Ken, "Aren't you going to do something?"

"What's it to do with me? It's their fight," Ken calmly replied.

"Ken, make them stop. Someone might get hurt."

Ken gave me a look that said, *You asked for it.*

He made a flying leap to join the ruckus. Now three bodies, all in their Sunday suits, rolled around in the snow, grunting and groaning, arms and legs all entangled. Alex just stood beside me, looking on, slightly bored with the whole scene.

After a minute or two, the three of them were back on their feet. Ken stood between Rob and Peter, holding their collars.

"You've both been hit in the head, so now you're even," he reasoned.

With flared tempers fading, Peter softly grumbling, Rob's red face still glaring, they brushed the snow off their suits and reluctantly united to search the snow for the eyeglasses. Once they were found and dried off, they pushed the car out of the snowbank—this time with everyone's help.

As I walked into the house for lunch, I pondered over what had happened. Coming from a family of girls, this was all new to me. I wasn't used to this alpha male manoeuvring. As no bloody noses or broken bones occurred, I decided this was the way men solved disagreements. It was over quickly and was more exciting than the female squabbles at my house.

———

Our family suffered from an affliction Linda and I called the Glendenning Curse. No matter what time we left for an appointment, we'd always arrive ten minutes early. The curse resulted in kicking our heels in waiting rooms longer than necessary and arriving too early for dinner at our friends' homes. It was normal to sit in the car around the corner and wait for the appropriate time to arrive.

Ken didn't have this problem—quite the opposite. He was always late. Ken didn't own a wristwatch and lacked the sense of the passing of time. He thought he could shower, stop at the bank, wash his car, and get his hair trimmed all within twenty-five minutes. Because I was usually early, the problem was compounded. If we'd arrange for Ken to arrive at 7:00 p.m., he might not arrive until 7:45 p.m. This left me waiting for an hour because I'd already been fifteen minutes early. However, I noticed one discrepancy: he never showed up late for a hockey game and rushed around in a panicked frenzy to avoid making the team wait.

One frosty Friday night, I reached the limit of my endurance and decided to drive myself to a young adult church service we had planned to attend together. I asked Mom to tell Ken, when he finally arrived, that I'd left and would meet him there. She was reluctant but didn't have a choice after I drove off.

When Ken arrived at church, sometime later, I explained that I had places to go and people to see and didn't want to waste my time waiting around. Judging by the remorseful look on his face, I knew he at last understood. Afterward he made a conscious effort to be punctual, but I didn't know to what extent until a few months later.

On a spring Saturday morning, Dad looked out the front window of our house to see Ken sitting in his car with a police car pulled up behind him. This was unusual in our quiet neighbourhood and upset Dad as he wondered what crime Ken had committed to warrant police involvement. My family gathered by the window, peering around the curtain and, from where we watched, it looked like Ken received a ticket.

After the officer left and Ken knocked on the door, I asked what had happened. He said the ticket was for going through a stop sign, but I pointed out that our street didn't have one. Evidently the officer had pulled him over a few blocks away, but Ken had requested that he follow his car to my house so I'd know he had arrived on time. Ken said the police officer was very understanding and had a girlfriend like me, too.

Occasionally Ken was still late, but it wasn't the chronic problem it had been.

———

Ken liked fast muscle cars and usually had several in various stages of disrepair—I mean, restoration—that he and Rob were working on. I spent most Saturday afternoons dressed up in a spare pair of Ken's greasy, smelly coveralls, peering under a hood, passing Ken ratchet tools and torque wrenches as he sprawled underneath on his creeper. When he asked for the hammer and I heard the clanging ring of metal on metal, I knew he was especially frustrated with an uncooperative bolt. While grunting, he'd explain the mystical intricacies of engines, the explanation punctuated with words like timing chains, internal combustion, cam shafts, power trains, rocker arms, and pistons. I enjoyed just being together, listening to the sound of his rumbly voice.

Being a good, steady driver, Ken never took unnecessary risks, content to wait for the traffic to clear—sometimes waiting for an excessively long time—before changing lanes to overtake a slow-moving truck. This was true while he drove his pickup. He also had an old diesel Mercedes sedan, and when he drove it I swear he'd transform into my personal chauffeur, escorting me around town, complete with a British accent, who insisted on opening my car door for me.

But once he slid behind the wheel of his 1969 Cougar convertible, donned his leather cap, and put down the top, he changed into another character—one who resembled the hoodlum I'd witnessed years earlier. The engine revved, the wheels spun, and we'd take off like a shot, accompanied by the squeal of tires. The change in him and his driving style, depending on which car keys he held in his hand, always intrigued me.

The highlight of Ken's winter was to escape on a weekend ski trip with his buddies, giving him a few days packed with adventure and camaraderie. You wouldn't choose the word finesse to describe how Ken skied; he attacked the hill, treating it like a challenge to be conquered. While others chose the easy route, Ken searched for the most treacherous part of every trail. The green trails marked on the map were for sissies while the black diamond trails mocked him like a red flag does a bull. If a *double* black diamond trail existed, this is where you'd find him. He took what the hill threw in his path and skied away like a warrior who had just conquered his enemy, quite often with one arm raised above his head in victory.

I followed Ken down the hill when we skied together, so I quickly improved and was able to keep up. (Though he probably held back when I was with him.) He used long skis, but I chose shorter skis than I should have to enable me to more easily manoeuvre through the moguls. The drawback was not being able to coast very far on the flat runs, so I would hold the end of Ken's ski pole as he towed me along behind him.

We were always on the go. We tobogganed on the hill behind Ken's house, ice-skated at City Hall, skied whenever we could, snowmobiled over hills, rode our bikes, swam till we were blue from cold, hiked along the Bruce Trail, canoed on peaceful lakes, water skied until our legs shook from exhaustion, and walked hand in hand over brightly coloured fallen leaves.

How was I to know this would all be impossible in a few years? Even walking hand in hand would be nothing but a memory. Perhaps if I had known I'd have treasured these days more carefully.

Chapter Three

THE BIG MOMENT

A fter dating for about two years, we started talking about purchasing a house together. Mortgage interest rates were very high, at thirteen percent, so we thought it wise to purchase a house needing renovations. Since Ken was handy at repairs, we could take advantage of lower selling prices by doing the work ourselves. We called these deals "fix-'em-up specials."

After casually looking for a couple of months, God led us to the perfect house. The sturdy, red brick bungalow sat on a little over an acre of land with a detached two-car garage. A large willow tree shaded the house, a double row of pine trees marched along the horseshoe-shaped driveway, raspberry bushes grew in the backyard, and a cherry tree kept company with a currant bush. The extra land would easily store Ken's tools and construction equipment and the price was right. Our offer was accepted with very little haggling. As I write, I'm enjoying the view from my office window of this same house.

We put every cent we'd saved into the down-payment to reduce the monthly payments and now needed to save up some money to buy furniture and appliances. We viewed credit cards as something to be used while traveling or for emergencies. So the house stood empty while we slowly fixed it up. Everything had to be done—windows replaced, damp basement repaired, carpets ripped out, driveway resurfaced, garage doors replaced, wallpaper stripped off and then walls painted... the list went on and on. We did all the work ourselves on the weekends and in the evenings after we'd worked all day at our regular jobs. The house was located between each of our parents' houses, so we met there most evenings.

Even though we hadn't set a wedding date, I anticipated an engagement ring soon. However, Ken seemed to be on a different timetable. I was on edge, watching for hints, waiting for the "big moment"—but it didn't arrive. Christmas, Ken's twenty-third birthday, Valentine's Day, Easter, and my twenty-first birthday all came and went with no ring.

Finally, six months after purchasing the house, I broached the subject, hinting that if we married late in the fall we could book a ski trip for our honeymoon. By the light that shone in his eyes, I could tell this idea had caught his imagination. His look said, *What better way is there to begin a marriage than on a ski trip?*

Now I really anticipated the big moment to happen soon.

A few weeks after this conversation, Ken invited me to a fancy restaurant for dinner. After eating a special meal, he held my hand across the table and I looked deep into his eyes, waiting for his words of undying love and devotion, but the conversation just meandered along, not moving anywhere special.

After rising from the table, Ken helped me with my jacket and asked if I wanted to walk in the restaurant's beautiful garden. Of course I readily agreed, and we walked hand in hand under the trees, along the Credit River. Still no ring. After he drove me home in his old pickup, I was disappointed and frustrated. He was certainly testing my patience!

A typical outing for us on a Friday night was the stock car races at Sunset Speedway. We were meeting friends there and then afterward continuing to the cottage to spend time with my family.

After a long day, I felt drowsy as we drove north. I let my eyes close and relaxed against the back of the seat. In that in-between stage, not asleep but not completely awake, I heard the rustling of a paper bag. Opening one eye, I saw Ken bend over while driving and take a small package out from under his seat. He set it on the dashboard.

I closed my eye and feigned sleep even though I was now wide awake. Did I dare to hope? Was this the moment I had been waiting for? Could I be wrong again? I remembered a small detail that I hadn't previously taken notice of. When we'd parked the truck at the racetrack earlier, Ken had been unusually concerned that I had locked my door. In fact, I couldn't ever remember him locking the doors of his old truck before.

Against my better judgment, hope started to rise. But wait—after the loud, smelly stock car races? This wasn't very romantic!

He slowed the truck and pulled over under a tree in front of a small white church. That's when I knew the big moment had arrived. He was apprehensive when he told me he loved me and asked me to be his wife. His nervousness touched me. Throwing my arms around his neck, I said yes, and I still wear his diamond ring today. He told me later that, because he'd sprained his ankle a few days earlier and couldn't go to work, he'd finally had time to go shopping for a ring. When I returned to the jeweller to have the ring sized, the sales clerk remembered Ken and told me how cute he had looked choosing a ring while leaning on his crutches. I have never been so thankful for a sprained ankle!

My family joyfully accepted the news, admired the ring, and began planning an intimate Christmas wedding. Mom sewed my gown, Dad gave me away, and Linda was one of my bridesmaids. Ken's Dad and Mom provided a vanload of red poinsettias. Rob was Ken's best man, while Peter and Alex were his groomsmen. It rained on our wedding day, but all my dreams were coming true.

For our honeymoon, we flew to Vancouver, British Columbia, rented a car, and drove to Whistler for a week of skiing. The trip was a perfect start to the rest of our lives together.

When we returned home Ken carried me over the threshold. One year after purchasing our house, we were moved in. We still hadn't completed the improvements it needed, but now we called it home.

Two years later, in 1987, Ken was best man when Rob married Carey. They rented a cute house next door to ours and lived there for about a year before moving to Georgetown. The guys removed part of the fence between our houses so we could easily walk back and forth between our back doors. Because we didn't own a TV, we went to their house to watch old movies; and because they didn't have a clothes dryer, they used ours, dropping odd socks out of the hamper along the way. When Carey had dinner ready and couldn't find Rob, she'd phone our house asking me to send him home, and quite often I called her to do the same thing for me. It got to the point when the visiting brother would hear the telephone ring, jump up, and run home, pretending he had already been on his way. Our lives resembled *The Flintstones*, where Fred and Barney made excuses to Wilma and Betty to try smoothing over their latest predicament.

My sister, Linda, and Ken's youngest brother, Alex, had been dating for a while and also decided to get married. Two sisters marrying two brothers was unusual in our circle of friends, but it didn't seem unusual to us. Alex fit right into my family, as Linda did into Ken's, and Alex grew to become like a true brother to me.

———

After Ken and I had been married for about two and a half years, I felt the time had come to start thinking about having a baby. When we'd first married, we had decided to pay off our mortgage first so I could be a stay-at-home mom. Our mortgage was coming up for renewal in the next few months, and I calculated we'd have saved enough to pay it off.

Some of you reading this may wonder how we could afford to do this at such a young age. However, we purchased our house before real estate values increased dramatically, and each year we made it a priority to make lump-sum payments on the mortgage. We paid cash for everything, didn't take expensive vacations, drove older vehicles, and watched how we spent every dollar. Even eating out was a rare luxury. We both believe the Lord put this desire in our hearts because He already knew what the future had in store for us.

With the end of mortgage payments in sight, I sat down with Ken and broached the subject of starting a family. I didn't really expect any opposition and was surprised when Ken's face reflected uneasiness. He didn't have any concrete objections, and the reasons for his hesitation seemed vague. Remembering how reluctant he had been to get engaged and set a wedding date, I realized that he became hesitant, even fearful, to make changes when he was happy and content with the way things were. Ken believed that parenthood came with a mountain of responsibility and shouldn't be rushed into without careful consideration. We were extremely happy together, our marriage was a success, we loved our home, Ken's business was doing well, and we enjoyed the cottage in the summers and a ski trip each winter. This was a life-changing decision and a lifetime commitment; once a child is born, you can't give it back.

Ken never said, "No, now is not the time." But he also couldn't bring himself to say, "Yes." He finally admitted that he found it hard to breathe when we talked about it, that he needed time to get used to the idea. I caught him off-guard by asking how much time he needed. He paused, looked a little confused, and said he needed one month.

Ah, now we were getting somewhere.

I got up from the table, grabbed a pen, flipped the calendar over to the next month, and put a circle around the date exactly thirty days later. We decided that he could think about it and get used to the idea, and then we'd continue the conversation.

I kept my promise and didn't mention it again. Only once, about halfway through, I pointed to the circled date and asked him if he was thinking about what he was supposed to. He swallowed hard, turned a little white, and said that he was.

Like in fishing, patience is everything.

On the appointed day, after I had cooked his favourite meal, Ken reluctantly agreed to start a family.

About nine months later, we were blessed with a perfect, nine-pound-three-ounce baby boy. We named him James Kenneth. He had chubby cheeks, fat little legs, and blond, eiderdown hair. He was a happy, easy baby and Ken took to fatherhood like a fish to water. No one could have known how scared and timid he'd been ten months earlier. He changed diapers, warmed bottles, and carried James with him wherever he went, under his arm like a football. Our small, two-bedroom house was now full and Ken started a large project on the front of the house, adding a solarium to give us more room.

Twenty-one months after James was born, Jonathan William joined our family. He had a rosebud mouth, long legs, and loved to be cuddled.

With John's arrival, we needed another bedroom, so Ken decided to add a half-story to our house. He barely had one project finished before starting the next one. His days were busier than ever with projects on the go at work and also at home, not to mention two little boys to love.

Ken was a fabulous father, stepping into the role as naturally as he stepped into his work boots each morning. James always woke up early, at about 5:30 a.m., to ensure he could say goodbye to Ken before he left for work.

After an exhausting day, Ken had the patience to tote James along wherever he went. When James was about three and John was about one and a half, I looked out my kitchen window to see Ken slowly and patiently pushing a wheelbarrow across the backyard. It was filled with dirt and on each side was a small boy clutching the side, each thinking they were helping, with Ken's stride shortened to match theirs. On the return trip, with the wheelbarrow empty, the boys were treated to a bumpy ride back, sitting one in front of the other, each laughing and holding on. It didn't matter to Ken that his project took two or three times longer this way—he always included the boys.

After a snowfall, Ken shovelled pathways in the backyard in a maze pattern for James to follow. This entertained James for hours, until he was too cold to stay out any longer, walking along, following in the footprints left by his dad. Each spring, with the resurrection of the riding lawnmower, Ken cut grass with a small boy sitting on each knee. Ken's feet controlled the speed, James steered, and John clutched Ken's shirt, holding on tightly.

Ken climbed the tall willow tree in our yard and hung a swing for the boys. We had the tallest swing for miles around. The arc was so wide that my stomach did flip-flops, like on an amusement park ride. Most of the boys' friends were too scared to use it.

At the cottage, when the water was warm enough, Ken strapped life jackets on the boys and they spent weekends swimming, jumping in the water, riding in the boat, or tinkering around. We have hours of home movie footage Ken recorded during these years.

Just as Ken was a faithful father, he was also faithful in his church attendance. We had a regular routine worked out. Ken would drop me off at the church door and I'd go straight to the five-year-old Sunday school class where I taught. Then he would park the car and carry the boys to their own classes, one under each arm. Ken and I wanted to instill in our own young family the same values each of us had been raised with.

I remember a conversation Ken and I had before he went to work one day. We talked about how happy we were, how much God had blessed us with our young sons and with our home. I confessed to Ken that I felt afraid, afraid of something bad happening, that this couldn't last—I was too happy. Ken reassured me that no matter what happened in the future, God would be with us.

Chapter Four

LIFE TAKES A TURN

The receptionist at Toronto Western Hospital said Ken was in Neuro ICU on the fourth floor. What was Neuro? Like in neurology? Wasn't that having to do with the brain and spinal cord? ICU? As in intensive care unit? I was afraid. I wanted to be cowardly, turn around, and run home. When I had said goodbye to Ken yesterday—was it only yesterday?—our reunion wasn't supposed to be at a hospital, in an intensive care unit.

Alex, Linda, and I couldn't remember the receptionist's directions and fumbled our way to ICU.

When I stepped into the waiting room, someone said, in a strained voice, "Sharon is here."

I was the last one to arrive. Everyone was already there—Ken's parents and my parents, Rob and Peter, close friends, a pastor from our church, everyone except Carey, who was at home expecting her third child.

All heads turned towards me. The atmosphere was thick and heavy, oppressive.

I thought we'd arrived too late and blurted out, "Has he died?"

Rob shook his head and let me know that he had just gathered everyone together to give a brief update. Ken had hurt his neck, was scheduled for a CT scan, and this was all he knew so far.

The hours slowly ticked by—one by one, each hour lasting an eternity. We watched other people come, stay for a while, then leave again, but no one came to tell us the extent of Ken's injuries, how he was doing, or even if he was conscious.

It was well past dinnertime, about 8:30 p.m., when Rob left to inquire about local hotels so I could stay close by for the night. In the hospital lobby, he paused by the desk of a volunteer who saw his frustration and asked if he was okay. Rob told her he was not okay and explained about waiting for so many hours without hearing anything. She was a young girl and didn't know what to do, but she had a list of phone numbers with the name and number of the head surgeon of the neurological ward. She gave the number to Rob on the condition he not reveal who had given it to him.

He dialled the head surgeon and explained how long we'd waited without hearing an update. The surgeon assured Rob that someone would be by soon to give us a report, and that he should return to the waiting room.

The call got the ball rolling and in a few minutes a nervous-looking intern with several pens stuck in the front pocket of his white coat came out to speak with us. I knew this would be my only chance that day to find out about Ken's condition, so I made the conscious decision to not get upset, no matter what he said, but detach myself emotionally, postponing my reaction so I could concentrate on getting all the facts.

The intern didn't ask me to take a seat. He didn't soften the blow with kind words but came straight to the point: Ken had broken his neck. His fifth and sixth vertebrae were severely broken and also dislocated. By making a fist and moving his fingers, he demonstrated with his knuckles how the dislocated vertebrae looked. Ken's spinal cord was pinched, and probably damaged, which had resulted in his legs being paralyzed and leaving very little movement in his arms. He explained that they were trying to stabilize his spine using a halo and traction and were hoping the vertebrae would move back into place on their own. Ken also had a badly broken right arm and a collapsed lung, but these weren't a priority in his care at the moment.

He stopped talking and I assumed he had finished his report. I asked if Ken's life was in danger and the intern explained that his condition was very unstable—and that it would remain unstable until his spinal cord was stabilized. He told me that I could see him soon.

Then he disappeared, returning to wherever he had come from.

I hadn't let the intern's words sink in while he was speaking, because I wanted to stay alert to absorb all the facts, but now his words replayed in my mind. Ken had broken his neck, Ken's legs were paralyzed, Ken's life was unstable, Ken could *die*. It was unreal, unimaginable, that Ken could be paralyzed. He was only thirty-one years old, the most active person I knew. The word "broken" sounded so final. Was this permanent? What did this mean for our family? Would James and John never feel their father's arms around them again? What did this mean for me? Was I to become Ken's nurse instead of his wife? Was I now married to a quadriplegic? Could we ever be normal again? Would he die, making me his widow?

Ignorance was better than this! I wished I could somehow turn back the clock. I sank into a chair beside my sister. We put our arms around each other and wept. Everyone else was in shock, too, finding it hard to comprehend.

Soon afterward, everyone gathered around me in a tight circle to pray for Ken. I felt ashamed, because this annoyed me. How could everyone gather calmly and pray in hushed tones when my whole world had fallen apart? No, not fallen apart—had been violently ripped apart at the seams. Emotions were bubbling up, ready to burst out, and I feared I couldn't control them any longer. I wanted to scream and kick, to let myself go and lose control.

Desperate for privacy, there was nowhere private to go.

While they calmly prayed, I walked out of the waiting room and paced back and forth in the hallway. Anger surmounted my ability to control it and I kicked the concrete wall, pounding it with my fists. It felt good to physically vent the turmoil I was going through. Questions filled my mind, but I had no answers. Longing for this terrible nightmare to end, I wanted to fast-forward to the future—to a time when I had answers to the questions swirling around me. Even though I was surrounded by people who loved me and were there to support me, I felt alone. Who was I to turn to?

About eight months earlier, I had hit a deer with my car. It had been upsetting for me, because the deer was badly injured, suffering for quite a while before finally dying on the side of the road. Afterward, when I arrived home with a piece of the car's broken grill still clutched in my hand, Ken had been so kind and tender. He'd stood there and held me while I cried, not asking too many questions, never criticizing my driving, not getting upset over the damage to the car. He just held me.

That's what I wanted him to do now, to come stand beside me, to comfort me. No one else would do. I wanted to feel his stubbly cheek against mine and hear his deep, husky voice close to my ear murmuring that it was all right. The one person I wanted to hold me couldn't—he was down the hall in a sterile room, paralyzed, fighting for his life.

I turned to the only one I knew who could help me, the only one I knew who understood, the only one I knew whose arms were strong enough to carry me—I turned to Jesus. Kneeling in the middle of the hallway, I pleaded with God to give me the strength to face the future. I bargained that if God wanted to take Ken's legs, I would learn to live with that, but I begged Him not to take his arms—for James' and John's sake—so Ken could hug them again. Never have I prayed such a prayer of anguish and pleading in my life, and I hope I will never have to again.

Finally, when the turmoil started to recede, my prayer was simply "God, please help me! I need you like never before."

When facing difficult situations in the past, I had relied on my own strength until the crisis passed. The Lord had always been first, but I hadn't let Him sit in the driver's seat of my life. Now I needed Him to take control of the steering wheel, because crawling into the back seat and hiding on the floor was all I was capable of.

For the first time, I couldn't cope on my own. I needed His support at a whole new level. How do you totally rely on God when the rug has been pulled out from under your feet and you find yourself sitting on the floor?

The questions I'd been asking God slowly started to turn into statements, like someone was sitting on my shoulder whispering into my ear: *You'll have to take out the garbage every week from now on.*

"Is this true?" I asked God.

I felt His answer. He was right there beside me, but He only said, "Trust Me."

You'll have to drive a van so a wheelchair can fit inside. You hate driving vans.

Again I asked God if this was true and His reply was simply, "Trust Me."

You can say goodbye to Christian school for your boys. Now the voice had a mocking tone.

"Trust Me."

You'll be changing bedpans for the rest of your life. You never signed up for this.

"Trust Me."

Back and forth this went, round and round, over and over, like a buzzing in my head I wished would stop. I'm the kind of person who looks reality squarely in the face, eye to eye, without flinching. I was afraid that my strong husband, the man I depended on, would become dependent on me for everything. That Ken would no longer be my anchor but my shackle. That the independence I had just started to feel again as my babies grew into boys would be taken away forever. That I would become a slave to Ken's physical needs.

My enemy, Satan, was painting a vivid picture of my future, showing me in living colour how drab and hopeless it would be. Where was God? I wanted Him to draw up a chair, sit down beside me, take my hand, and tell me in detail how the story ended—to tell me all the plans He had for me. But all He said was, "Trust me."

Two words. Nothing more.

I had always lived my life by the Boy Scout motto: "Be Prepared." I planned ahead, ready for any eventuality. Now what was I to do? There was no way anyone could prepare for this. Maybe God wasn't revealing the future because He didn't want me to worry about what the future held, but to concentrate on getting through the next hour.

The realization slowly dawned on me that the only way to survive was to deal with it one moment at a time, to concentrate on what needed my attention in the current hour and leave the rest in God's hands. This wasn't a lesson I learned in an instant but one I needed to relearn again and again. It took me weeks, even months, to fully understand what it means to "trust God."

I returned to the waiting room and sat down, exhausted, searching my purse for a dry Kleenex. Everyone was wrapped in their own emotions. No one knew what to do, what to say.

Rob flopped down beside me, put his feet up on the chair opposite, and crossed his arms. He didn't need to say it; his body did. He would stay with me through the duration. If I needed his assistance, he'd be there.

We all sat together, waiting for permission to see Ken. People spoke in hushed tones, nervous laughter erupting once in a while. Someone found a newspaper and slowly flipped the pages. Rob kept changing chairs, chatting to whoever was nearby. Ken's mom calmly read a New Testament she kept in her purse. Linda kept blowing her nose. I just sat watching the room. We felt so helpless.

Even though I'd been waiting for hours, I was caught off-guard when Rob told me I could finally go in and see Ken.

Wait! I didn't want Ken to see me tear-stained with messy hair and a red nose. I didn't want him to know how upset I was.

There was a small washroom nearby with a mirror. I splashed my face with cool water, dried it with a scratchy brown paper towel and searched through my purse for something I could use to help. I applied a bit of lipstick, used my comb, and then inhaled deeply and examined myself again in the mirror. Two brown eyes looked back at me from a pale face which made my newly applied lipstick look too vibrant. I admitted defeat and zipped up my purse.

Oh well, I thought. *Ken won't really care anyway. He probably won't even notice.*

I hadn't fixed myself up for his sake, but to help bolster my courage to face the unknown waiting at the end of the hallway.

Rob opened the heavy double doors and we followed the signs directing us through the Cardiac ICU to the Neuro ICU. The uncertainty of what faced me at the end of the stark hallway made me feel like I had weights strapped to each foot. I didn't want to go, but I forced myself to face what lay ahead.

Rob could sense I was wavering and took my hand, wordlessly supporting me. He was also apprehensive about seeing Ken, remembering all the smeared blood he had witnessed earlier. He told me years later that he had thought he was taking a soon-to-be widow to say her last goodbye to her dying husband.

Finally, we reached the door to Ken's room and, before stepping in, I took a deep breath and stuck a smile on my face. More than anything else, I wanted to be strong for Ken, for him to know I'd be there for him.

He was lying flat on his back, nurses had washed his face clean, and the halo was attached to his head by pins, one centred above each eyebrow, poking into his forehead. A steel cable ran from the top of the halo to the head of his bed then through a pulley mounted on the wall with weights suspended above the floor. He was surrounded by tubes and wires, all hooked into various beeping machines, some with graphs monitoring each heartbeat.

In the midst of all this, two blue eyes sought out mine. Our eyes locked, and my fake smile turned into a real one as I watched a slow, guilty-looking, boyish grin spread across his face. He wordlessly asked me a question by raising one eyebrow, wondering if he was in trouble and if I was angry with him. Of all the scrapes he'd been in before, this one topped them all.

But instead of anger, relief washed over me. He was alert, knew me, and seemed his usual cheerful self with no sign of a brain injury. How much of this cheerfulness was an act for my benefit? I didn't know. We were both trying to keep as much heartache away from the other as we could.

I asked him how he felt and if he was in pain, and he said that he hurt everywhere. Looking back, I realize that he minimized its degree at the beginning.

Seeing Ken so helpless—machines beeping and buzzing around him, his nurse constantly monitoring his IV lines—overwhelmed my senses. After only a few minutes, the stress escalated. I felt faint and had to quickly step into the hallway, taking some deep breaths to refresh myself. After doing this a couple of times, I decided to escort family members from the waiting room, one by one, so they could have a brief moment with him. This gave me an excuse to take frequent breaks, and the visitors took Ken's mind off his pain.

He greeted everyone with a smile, and quite often offered a small word of encouragement as he didn't want anyone to worry or lose sleep over him. This made it obvious he wasn't aware of the extent of his injuries. If it was me lying there, I'd be asking every nurse and doctor exactly what was wrong with me. I'd ask to see the X-rays myself and want my chart read to me. But I knew this wasn't Ken's way. I protected him from knowing the truth. There would be plenty of time in the days ahead to have that painful conversation.

After each of the family had a quick one- to two-minute visit, I gave him a kiss goodbye and told him we'd see him in the morning. I gave his nurse my hotel phone number in case there were any changes in the night, and then left him to rest.

Back in the waiting room, Ken Mercer asked me if I wanted something to eat. I couldn't remember when I had eaten last, but discovering I was hungry I requested a bowl of soup. It was now very late, and I don't know from where that soup was conjured up, but it sure tasted good. I can still remember it, cream of leek, thick and warm and tasty, with a big plastic spoon to eat it with.

After the warm soup, exhaustion stepped up and put its heavy arm around my shoulders. I was glad Rob had reserved a hotel room nearby for Linda and I, and that Ken wouldn't be far away. We were dropped off at the hotel and checked in, asking for two toothbrushes and toothpaste as we didn't have any luggage.

In the elevator, while ascending to our room, I asked Linda not to cry again. If she weakened, then I would, and I was too tired for further tears. She agreed with me and we decided to tough it out, to keep our emotions in check and get ready for bed as quickly as possible. There was the possibility that, if Ken was to regress, we could be summoned back to the hospital.

Lying between fresh, crisp sheets in the darkness, waiting for sleep to find me, I remembered my morning devotions at the cottage. The devotion was in a little booklet entitled *Our Daily Bread* and I still have it, now yellowed with age. It was about the great composer Ludwig van Beethoven and his fear of his encroaching deafness. He had been afraid that it would hinder his ability to compose music of lasting value. After consulting doctors and trying every possible remedy, the deafness had continued to increase until all hearing was gone. To everyone's amazement, though, some of Beethoven's greatest music was written after he was totally deaf. The devotion ended with:

Child of God, have you experienced a great loss? Don't lose hope. Call on the Lord. Trust Him and keep listening. If you do, you will gain even from loss.[1]

It was based on a verse written by David: *"Let the morning bring me word of your unfailing love, for I have put my trust in you"* (Psalm 143:8).

David's prayer became my own prayer, asking God to show me His unfailing love in the morning while I put my trust in Him. Peace settled over me like a warm blanket. My tense body relaxed, and sleep granted me the rest I craved.

---

[1]   Henry G. Bosch, "Gaining from Losing," *Our Daily Bread* (Grand Rapids, MI: Radio Bible Class, 1993), Volume 34, August 9.

Chapter Five

OUR LAST FAREWELL?

W aking up early, I called the hospital before getting out of bed to check on Ken's progress. The nurse said that Ken had had a good night with no changes from last evening. Relief swept over me and I breathed a prayer of thanks to God.

As Linda and I ordered breakfast in the hotel's sunny restaurant, I couldn't help but remember the last time I had eaten breakfast downtown. It had been with Ken eight years earlier, at the Royal York Hotel, the morning after our wedding night.

Linda remarked, while glancing over the restaurant, that we don't know what others are going through by their outward appearance, and I agreed. If someone looked our way, they wouldn't know I was in the midst of the greatest crisis of my life.

After breakfast, we stood outside on the bright sidewalk, waiting for Peter to drive us to the hospital, and I wondered what this new day would bring.

———

By now, we knew our way around and went straight to the Neuro ICU waiting room. I had slept deeply for several hours, eaten a hot breakfast, and felt much better than when I had left. I looked forward to seeing Ken without the apprehension of the day before. Mom, Dad, and Ken's family started to arrive and were allowed to visit Ken right away.

When I slipped in beside his bed, he greeted me with a big smile. Seeing him looking a little better, and noticing the slightly improved movement in his left arm, encouraged me and caused a seed of hope to slowly grow like a fragile green shoot. I thanked God that He had answered my prayer by showing me His unfailing love in the morning. Maybe Ken would recover. Maybe my life wasn't going to be so bleak after all.

I didn't realize then that this frail new hope would be crushed so quickly.

Ken's medical team observed him closely. Every few hours his spine was X-rayed to monitor the traction to ensure the vertebrae were moving back into alignment.

By the afternoon, a doctor brought bad news. The traction on Ken's halo wasn't working and the likelihood of his death was still as great as the evening before. He was referred to a neurological surgeon who would operate to stabilize him. The surgeon, Dr. Fehlings, came out to the waiting room and explained that he would perform an anterior cervical fusion, realigning Ken's spine using plates and screws. The fifth, sixth, and seventh vertebrae in his neck would be fused together using bone removed from Ken's hip. The eight-hour marathon operation was scheduled for 7:00 p.m. that evening. Dr. Fehlings would head up the first team, then another team of surgeons would take over to finish up. He also explained that any error on his part could cause additional damage to the spinal cord, resulting in further paralysis.

I'll never forget Dr. Fehlings standing there in his white coat, concern reflected in his face, explaining that this type of procedure was a "major, major operation, very similar to brain surgery" and the possibility of death was very real. However, without the surgery, Ken couldn't live.

Dr. Fehlings wasn't nervous and jittery, like the intern I'd first met, but exuded a reassuring confidence. He took his time with us, ready to answer our questions. I found out later that he was world-renowned, the top surgeon in his field.

The family gathered together, and with the surgeon's permission Ken's mom prayed over his hands. We then settled ourselves for another long evening of waiting.

Sitting in the same chair as the evening before, I found myself dealing with the same fears, the same worries. The same people gathered together in the same waiting room—again. The new day had brought new hope. God had answered my prayer, as the morning had brought me good news. Ken had been slightly improved, the movement in his arms slightly better.

But now where was God? Why was I being pushed back into the depths of despair I had just managed to crawl out of? How could I possibly endure another evening as bad as the previous one?

Reluctantly, Rob called the hotel a second time to reserve another room.

Rob Doubts

The closest person in my life was my brother Ken, perhaps even closer to me than my wife, Carey, because I'd known him my whole life. I wished Carey was here with me, but she was at home, expecting our third child. She was six months along and visiting hospitals wasn't a good idea for her. She was acting as our family's home base, giving updates on Ken's condition to the many people who called and relaying messages back to us.

After reserving another hotel room for Sharon and Linda, I went to a courtyard I had noticed earlier to be alone. It was warm there, so I sat on a bench in the shade and stretched my long legs onto the grass which was in bad need of watering. I wished I'd brought sunglasses to protect my eyes from the sun's glare, but also for privacy as I felt tears gathering, threatening to spill over.

I couldn't imagine life without Ken. We'd never been separated—not really. A few years earlier, I'd attended a college in Toronto, staying there during the week, but we'd spent most of our weekends together. We went to the same church, played together, and even worked together, running our construction company as business partners.

I wondered why I couldn't sense God's presence. Where was He? Why did I feel so empty and alone? Why were Ken's prospects so dark? This was not good—this was crap! I didn't have God's comfort, and I knew this was a problem. I had always thought God would be there when I needed Him. Asking God to swoop down, to comfort me with His presence, had resulted in nothing—just emptiness.

I was convinced Ken would die, that he was finished. I hadn't told anyone how I felt, especially not Sharon. Everyone else seemed to have faith that Ken would be okay, whatever that meant. I didn't want anyone to know how I felt because then I'd be the negative one—the guy with no faith. Then that little surgeon had come out and dropped the bombshell. I respected him for being honest and straightforward with us. He hadn't candy-coated anything, and for that I was grateful. He seemed to be more realistic than some of the others who were believing for a complete healing. Don't get me wrong; I believe God can heal someone in an instant if it's His will. Because I couldn't feel His divine presence myself, I believed the possibility of Him intervening with a healing was remote.

One thing I knew for sure: someone had to tell Ken this could be it—the end—that death was very near. I mentioned to Sharon that someone should tell him, but by the look of horror that crossed her face I knew I'd have to do it. If I had been the one lying on that hospital bed, I'd want to know the whole truth.

The problem was, how do you find the words to say, "Ken, you're going to die"? How could I verbalize this to my brother? I didn't know how I'd form the words, but I was sure I'd think of something when the time came. If worse came to worse, I'd just blurt it out—Ken would understand.

The shadows had slowly migrated and I was now sitting partway in the sun. I decided it was time to return to the waiting room.

A nurse said we could see Ken briefly before he was prepped for surgery. I asked Sharon to give me a few moments alone with Ken before coming into the room.

Sharon Says Goodbye

As I walked the long hall to Ken's ICU unit, I wondered how a wife says goodbye to her husband—her soulmate. The two of us might be about to share the last moment we would ever have together in this life. Ken knew I loved him. I'd said it countless times. Should I just repeat it? Those three oft-heard words, I love you, seemed inadequate to express the depth of my feelings, but at the same time they said it all. Love is such a simple word, only one syllable, to describe an emotion so deep, so steady. Love is much more than a fleeting emotion, it's solid, like a virtue or state of being. If Ken wasn't aware of the depth of my love by now, he never would.

I'd just settled down beside Ken when our good friend Paul, one of Ken's ski buddies, arrived. He hadn't visited Ken yet and was anxious to see him before surgery, even for just a few seconds. Ken was only allowed immediate family to visit, so I was surprised Paul had managed to get past the nurse on guard duty. It turned out Paul had told her he was a doctor, which was true, but he'd neglected to reveal that he practiced *veterinary* medicine.

Paul stood beside Ken's head and bent down close to him, so he could hear him better.

"Ken, how are you, buddy?" he asked. "Is there anything I can do for you?"

Ken said, "Yes, Paul. You can do one thing for me."

Paul didn't know what that could be and wondered if it was something big, like watching out for his kids in the future. He hesitated for a split second.

"Ken, I'll do anything," he said with conviction.

"Can you get out my skis and sharpen them for me?" Ken asked with a straight face.

Paul was dumbfounded, his mouth fell open, and he couldn't help but chuckle. Ken may be on his deathbed, but he certainly hadn't lost his sense of humour. After assuring Ken he'd sharpen his skis, Paul patted Ken's shoulder then quickly left the room, leaving us alone.

While I held Ken's hand, he told me that he knew the surgery was risky but not to worry, because he was ready for heaven. In fact, he was looking forward to being unconscious for a while as his pain was so great. We prayed together, I told him I loved him, gave him a quick kiss, stroked his cheek, and left his room.

My chest felt tight. I found it hard to breathe. My knees gave out and someone standing nearby caught me before I sank to the floor. Tears were inadequate to express the turmoil writhing inside me.

Someone unlocked a small, quiet room filled with worn furniture where I could be alone, away from anxious and curious eyes, with the freedom to lose control and kick a chair if I wanted to. With family around me, all dealing with their own pain and worry, I hesitated to vent my emotions publicly, afraid to add to their own distress. But instead of venting as I expected, I ended up just kneeling in front of an overstuffed chair, with my face buried in its lap, and cried out to God. I wanted to find my Rock, my Refuge, and run into my Strong Tower. Psalm 62:6–7 says, *"Truly he is my rock and my salvation; he is my fortress, I will not be shaken. My salvation and my honor depend on God; he is my mighty rock, my refuge."*

My crying slowly turned into a prayer—a desperate prayer—for God to come and help me, a prayer for God to preserve Ken's life, for God to allow Ken to hold out his arms and hug his boys once again.

My anguish only lasted for a few minutes and then something slowly started to change. Waves of peace washed over me, my heartrate slowed, my breathing became more regular, and I started to feel safe. God was answering the prayers of people who were praying for me. The Bible says in Deuteronomy 31:6 that He will never leave us, and I was now experiencing God's comforting presence, like I was protected in a strong tower.

Each and every time I have sought God's comfort, He has held me in His arms. Maybe He doesn't provide all the answers I seek, but He provides His perfect peace, the peace that surpasses our understanding described in Philippians 4:7.

I then knew God would walk beside me on this journey, hold my hand, and guide me in the days ahead. I left that shabby room a different person from the one who had walked in.

We still had hours to wait before we would hear an update, and sitting still any longer was impossible for me. Along with a pastor from our church, Rob and I found a long quiet hallway and walked back and forth, back and forth. I had never been one to pace, but once I started I couldn't stop. We paced nonstop for hours.

Around midnight, Dr. Fehlings left the operating room and joined us in the waiting room. We all stood up and I quickly scanned his face for any sign of grief—but none was written there. His face was open and assured. He brought the long anticipated news that the surgery had gone smoothly.

Relief audibly swept across the room. People murmured "Praise God" under their breath and collapsed into chairs, relieved. Smiles replaced frowns and everyone relaxed.

Dr. Fehlings said that Ken was very "messed-up inside." By this, he meant that Ken's spinal cord had suffered a lot of damage. His part was done, but there were still several hours of operating left while someone else finished and closed Ken up.

After hearing this, we decided to call it a night. Everyone went home while Linda and I returned to the hotel, this time carrying an overnight bag our family had brought for us.

Ken in Pain

The surgery didn't concern me as much as it did Sharon and Rob, because I was sure the surgeon would fix my broken bones and I'd head home soon. I was worried about Sharon, though, and what she was going through. She was being very brave and doing her best to smile and stay cheerful. All other concerns were driven from my mind, as dealing with the pain required my full concentration. If the anaesthetic granted me a few hours of relief, I wouldn't object. And if God called me home to heaven, I was ready. Actually, if I had to choose between living with this excruciating pain or heaven, I'd choose heaven—hands down.

I remembered when I was young, about ten or eleven, listening to a sermon about accepting Jesus Christ as Saviour. Afterward, with bowed heads, the preacher encouraged those who wanted to accept the invitation to raise their hands. I was surprised to see, out of the corner of my eye, Rob put up his hand. This was something I had never thought about before. In our home, Mom and Dad had modelled the Christian faith for us and taught us how to live a life dedicated to Christ, but I'd never paused to think about making this decision for myself.

Over the next few months, I pondered whether I needed to take this step of faith or just continue living as I had before. Would I just follow the lead of others by attending church on Sundays and listening to the Bible readings during family devotions, or would I embrace this faith and make it my own, make a personal decision to follow Christ? I concluded that, yes, my decision to serve Christ was a commitment I needed to make for myself, and I did just that. About two years later, Rob and I were baptized in water as an outward testimony of our commitment to be followers of Christ.

Sharon had just left when my nurse came in holding a clipboard. I was preparing to answer the usual list of questions when she caught me off-guard by saying I needed to sign a consent form for the surgery, and also sign to acknowledge that I was aware that my survival wasn't guaranteed. I looked at her, puzzled. How could I sign when my hands were paralyzed? She said marking an X would do. She put the pen between my fingers, encircled my hand with her own, and stroked two crude crossed markings on the signature line. She then started unhooking the wires and tubes attached to several machines and monitors. She explained I'd be taken over to surgery and prepped there.

An orderly rolled my stretcher into a plain white room where I was met by another nurse who held up a rubber tube and explained that she was going to put it up my nose and down my throat.

"That's impossible!" I said.

"Oh no, it's not."

"Oh yes, it is," I insisted.

She gave me some ice chips to chew on and put the flexible tube up my nose. While I was swallowing the chips, she eased it down my throat. I had been proved wrong! Then someone asked me to count to ten, like they do in the movies. I obediently started counting, but I only remember reaching three.

Muffled voices sounded a long way off. I squinted into a bright light and thought, *I'm alive.*

Opening my eyes fully was hard, as my face felt tight and swollen. The tube was still up my nose, I couldn't see the halo above my forehead anymore, and a tight neck brace rubbed against my chin.

Noticing that I was awake, a nurse said that she'd take the tube out of my nose. I didn't protest, but I should have. Taking it out felt like all the hair in my nose was ripped out. Unfortunately, I'm not bothered by a shortage of nose hair.

Disappointment overwhelmed me as acute pain filled my consciousness. The sensation felt different. Before, I had felt a constant, hard-to-pinpoint throbbing; now it was coming from specific areas in my body. My lower back felt like it had a knife in it.[2] My injured spinal cord was sending false signals to my brain from all over my body. The sensation felt brittle, tense, like a branch ready to snap. The pain medication, given every four hours, only served to take the edge off. In my case, it wasn't so much a painkiller as a pain diminisher—just making it bearable.

---

[2] I found out months later that removing the bone in my pelvis to repair my neck caused acute lower back pain which I'd have to endure for several years.

47

Chapter Six

LIFE IN ICU

At the hotel, I fell asleep more quickly than the previous night. God's peace still surrounded me. I felt His loving arms around me, drawing me closer and urging me to rest.

Jesus said in Matthew 11:28, *"Come to me, all you who are weary and burdened, and I will give you rest."* Jesus will grant rest for the souls of those who are tired, those who are overloaded by difficulties. Hebrews 4:10 says that *"anyone who enters God's rest also rests from their works, just as God did from his."* I love how this chapter in Hebrews refers to our salvation as rest. Because I had entered into God's rest by becoming a follower of Christ, I could rest in the finished work of what Christ did for us on the cross, resting in this assurance and not fretting about earning my way into heaven. God stands at His door of rest, inviting you in to share it with Him.

I accepted His invitation at a very young age—only four and a half years old—on a Sunday. Some may say I was too young to understand what I was doing, but after praying a simple prayer the change I felt was real and I understood exactly what I had done. A few hours earlier, my Sunday school teacher had explained to our class that, because of sin—the sin Adam and Eve committed and which still continues in us—our hearts are all black and dirty.[3] She had gone on to tell us that because Jesus had died on the cross and given His life as payment for our sin, all we had to do was accept His gift, invite Him into our lives, and He would make our hearts clean—sparkling white, like snow.

---

[3] Her class was for four-year-olds, so she used language we could understand.

After my mother had put me to bed for my nap that afternoon, I thought about what my teacher had said and felt my need for this cleansing. I folded my hands and prayed a very simple prayer, all by myself, asking Jesus to make my heart clean. Immediately I felt a difference. New joy bloomed and bubbled up within me, something I'd never felt before.

I had wanted to tell my mother and decided to risk being disciplined for getting up when I was supposed to be sleeping. She was in the kitchen, making herself a cup of tea at the counter, when I walked in and announced that I'd just asked Jesus into my heart. She shared my excitement and didn't hesitate to show her joy. We knelt down together at the living room couch to thank Jesus for what He'd just done for me.

Beginning in my early teens, and for decades afterward, I was involved in the children's ministry at my church, because I knew firsthand how a young child's life could be changed and transformed by God.

———

At 3:30 a.m., the phone rang, waking me up. It was the hospital calling to let me know that the surgery was over and Ken was in recovery, doing fine. I immediately fell back into a deep sleep, not waking again until 6:30 a.m. I called the hospital to get another update on Ken, then breathed a sigh of relief when I heard there was no change in Ken's movement as compared to before the surgery. The surgeon had fused Ken's spine without causing further damage to the fragile spinal cord. My verse, Psalm 143:8, came to mind again.

Later at the hospital, I found myself back in the waiting room, which had grown as familiar to me as my own living room. When I was allowed to visit Ken, I found his face swollen from the hours lying facedown during surgery. He had an eight-and-a-half-inch red incision on the back of his neck with a perfect row of evenly spaced metal staples holding the opening closed. The metal halo and weights were gone, replaced with a white plastic neck brace. Thankfulness flooded over me when I learned that, with the stabilization of Ken's spine, his life was more stable and not as precarious as the day before. We weren't out of the woods yet, but definitely on our way.

Ken seemed glad to see me but looked tired and lay quietly. He wasn't gifted at expressing his thoughts and feelings verbally; instead he expressed himself physically. After we were first married, when we lay in bed at night talking about our day, I noticed that Ken had difficulty describing his feelings with words. Sensing his frustration, I'd ask him which letter of the alphabet they most resembled. He'd pause, think about it, then name a letter. I'd inquire if it was in lowercase or uppercase, then trace the letter on his back or chest, demonstrating physically that I understood and empathized. This was our own unique way of communicating and empathizing with each other, unhindered by words—like soulmates sharing each other's thoughts without talking.

So, in intensive care, after seeing the pain etched on Ken's face, I asked him what letter best resembled what he was feeling. I then traced the letter on his chest, high enough so he could feel it. I'm sure our family and nurses thought we were slightly demented.

I thought about Ken's close waltz with death, and one thing became very apparent: I wanted Ken, the person who loved me wholeheartedly, who was easy to talk to and took the time to listen. The physical side of Ken, the one who skied and swam and skated, was secondary to who Ken was on the inside. This was the Ken I wanted, even if I had to accept a disability along with him.

Each ICU unit consisted of four beds, the occupants frequently changing. Ken received outstanding care, world-class, but this unit cared for the most critically ill patients, making the atmosphere heavy. Death lurked in the corner, never far away.

Time sped by while I sat with Ken because the nurses were busy around me. Something was always going on. But for Ken, time dragged. Each twenty-four-hour period was broken into four-hour segments, the frequency of his pain medication injections. His most oft-asked question was, "How long until my next pain shot?" It was difficult to tell him he still had several hours left to endure.

I no longer needed to stay at the hotel to be close to Ken, so I decided to return home for the night. My mom and dad came to stay with me so I wouldn't be alone. I missed James and John and was concerned they'd outstayed their welcome at the Rogers house. I'd been in touch and knew they were doing fine, were in fact enjoying the stay with their friends, but I missed them and wanted them close. I was a little apprehensive going to bed alone, but when I put my head on Ken's pillow, which still carried his scent, I fell into a deep, comforting sleep.

Over the weekend, my parents babysat while I travelled to the hospital. I also made arrangements for a babysitter to come to the house each day the following week. This freed me to take public transit each morning to spend the day with Ken, then return on the afternoon train to prepare dinner for the boys and spend the evening with them. They had never experienced daycare before, but Ken needed my attention more than they did right then.

———

Rob volunteered to travel by public transit with me the first time, as he used to live in the same downtown area and knew the route. The trip wasn't too complicated, but it involved taking the commuter train, then switching to the subway and finding the correct bus. The second day, with a backpack filled with what I'd need, I was on my own and found I had suddenly joined the commuter crowd. Downtown Toronto, with the roar of speeding buses and horns honking angrily, was like entering a different world after spending a couple of years quietly at home with young children. I didn't like the hustle and bustle, the jostling of the crowd. I reluctantly endured my commute each day.

As I sat on the bus, I couldn't help but ponder how quickly life can change and how much we take for granted. I wanted to stop the bicyclist to remind him to be thankful that he could pedal his bike with fully functioning legs. I wanted to interrupt the panting jogger to point out what a blessing his toned and muscular legs were. When I saw someone up a ladder, I wanted to call out, "Careful!" and remind them how easily accidents can happen.

I never blamed Ken for his injury or got angry with him. He wasn't the type of person to act rashly, without thinking, and I preferred to consider his fall as an unfortunate accident. Nothing could be gained by recriminations.[4]

———

The doctors and physiotherapists were still monitoring Ken's progress carefully. Someone had drawn a wide black line on Ken's chest with a marker pen, indicating exactly where his sensation of touch ended. It bothered me that this personal piece of information was made public, for anyone to see, and it was an almost rude reminder of the severity of his injury. After several days passed, I noticed another black line had been drawn about two inches lower.

Each morning I looked for further improvement, but no additional lines were drawn on Ken's chest. Drawing lines on someone's body may have been a callous thing to do, but it saved me from pestering Ken for daily updates.

Each day Ken's therapist turned back the bedclothes to uncover Ken's feet, took a large blunt pin, and pressed it against his toes, asking if he could feel the prick. It was painful to watch, because I knew how sensitive and ticklish Ken's feet normally were. He had a tough time putting on his own socks each morning because his foot jumped out of his hand if he accidentally touched a sensitive part. Now, if I wanted to, I could tickle his feet to my heart's desire and he'd not mind at all—which took all the fun out.

Ken still battled excruciating pain as his damaged spinal cord continued to send signals to his brain that something was wrong. Pinpointing the source was impossible for Ken because the sensation radiated from every area of his body. During the long nights, while Ken lay in the dim room waiting for the relief of sleep which never came, he softly sang or hummed old hymns he knew by heart—hymns he had sung in church hundreds of times, comforting favourites like "Amazing Grace"

---

[4] Weeks later, Rob talked to someone who had been present at the scene of Ken's accident and they said the way the ladder had lain on the ground, it looked like Ken had fallen off the ladder, that the ladder hadn't slipped first. This made us wonder if Ken, while standing on the ladder, had fainted from heat exhaustion.

and "What a Friend We Have in Jesus." These songs soothed him, encouraged him, and helped turn his mind away from his pain.

When he asked me to sing to him, I knew he'd reached his desperation point. I have difficulty carrying a tune and try to avoid singing solos. However, if it provided comfort, I'd willingly perform any feat Ken asked—even singing. Ken's most requested favourite was "Just a Closer Walk with Thee," which I found hard to sing, not because of my lack of talent but because the emotion it stirred up caused a lump in my throat. Bravely clearing the lump away, I sung it softly so just the two of us could hear, like a lullaby.

> Just a closer walk with Thee
> Grant it, Jesus, is my plea
> Daily walking close to Thee
> Let it be, dear Lord, let it be[5]

This prayerful hymn reminded me that our relationship with Jesus is more important than anything—even walking—and our life should be dedicated to a closer walk.

There was no night in ICU, even though the lights were dimmed. The sound of monitors beeping, ventilators breathing in and out for patients, heels clicking down the hallway, and muted voices all contributed to Ken's difficulty sleeping. It wasn't until after I arrived that he'd visibly relax. While I told him what our boys had been doing at home, he'd nod off. I'd then look questioningly at his nurse for reassurance that he was okay. She'd examine his monitor and whisper that he was finally in a natural sleep, usually the first time since the day before.

While he slept, I sat quietly beside his bed and continued my reading of *Pride and Prejudice*. Sometimes the book would slowly lower to my lap while I gazed at Ken, watching him sleep, wondering at our new circumstances. It was so unreal. Before, my days had been carefree as a young wife and mother focused on caring for her family. My main concern had been to be a good wife to my husband, raise my sons, and

---

[5] Author unknown.

decide what to cook for dinner. Now, without warning, my orderly life had turned upside down and I wasn't sure if the pieces would fit back together. I didn't even know if my new life would remotely resemble what I'd known before.

Once in a while Ken opened one eye, looking to see if I was still there, then let out a contented sigh and drift back to sleep. Until I discovered Ken couldn't sleep unless I was there, I hadn't realized that Ken's peace of mind depended on my presence in his life.

Ken still wasn't aware of the extent of his injury. Until the swelling went down in his spinal cord, we wouldn't know what permanent damage had been done, and unfortunately this usually took several months, sometimes even longer. Ken never asked what his prognosis was, so I kept it to myself, thinking he couldn't deal with much more right then.

As for me, I had no such reservations. Out of Ken's hearing, I asked the doctor detailed questions about Ken's condition and he'd take me into the hall, where a poster hung showing an internal diagram of the spine. There he'd patiently explain where Ken's injury was and the physical ramifications it could produce.

Each day in the early afternoon, after I fed Ken his lunch, I'd wake him up if he was sleeping (and he usually was) to say goodbye, because I was going to catch the train home. By this time I was quite tired, but I still had to deal with two energetic boys waiting for me.

Picking up our mail, I unexpectedly found notes and cards from my extended family and friends. Reading these notes became a highlight of my day as they each held a few lines of encouragement, reminding me that I wasn't alone and that people were praying for us daily.

Everyone kindly stepped in to offer support, and they frequently asked if there was anything they could do to ease my burden. Linda took charge of providing dinners. She rallied our friends, who each cooked and froze a dinner, then delivered them and loaded up my freezer. They were delicious home-cooked foods: soups, muffins, quiches, casseroles, chicken with rice. I'd select a dinner in the morning, put it in the fridge to thaw, then warm it when I got home. One girlfriend even sent over a complete turkey dinner with stuffing, gravy, mashed potatoes—the works. Recent events hadn't affected my appetite, and we ate like kings.

Later, freezing dinners became a ministry at our church headed up by Carey. For years afterward, our church kept a freezer full of home-made meals our pastors could access to deliver to those in need or families who were going through a rough time.

To help motivate Ken in his battle against the pain, we hung a few snapshots of James and John where he could easily see them. I didn't want the boys brought to ICU, so Rob made a video of Ken for them to watch at home so they'd know he was okay. A nurse helped Rob drape bedsheets over the equipment Ken was hooked to. They raised his bed until he was almost sitting upright, then recorded the cutest video for James and John. Ken said he loved them and missed them but had a broken arm and had to stay in the hospital so he could get better. At their young age, we thought they could better understand a broken arm than a broken neck. At the end of the video, Rob moved the camera close to Ken's mouth so he could "kiss" them.

The boys watched this video constantly, sitting in front of the TV on the floor. At each viewing, two-year-old John stood up and kissed Ken back, right on the TV screen. The video helped ease their longing to see their father.

The ICU unit had been Ken's home for one week until his collapsed lung returned to normal and his doctors felt he was stable enough to handle a second surgery to correct his broken right arm. When he fell, the point of his elbow had broken off and required some pins and fancy wirework to enable it to bend again.

This surgery was considered routine and, thankfully, lacked the drama of his first surgery. Everything went smoothly and Ken enjoyed a few more hours of pain-free unconsciousness. He was allowed to choose the colour of his fiberglass cast and chose a startlingly bright red one the exact colour of fresh blood. The first time I saw it, I took a second look, thinking he was bleeding profusely.

He recovered from this surgery so quickly that he was moved out of ICU to a ward on the fifth floor the next day. I anticipated this move and viewed it as the next step in his recovery, but instead it proved to be a depressing disappointment.

Chapter Seven

BILLBOARD OF FEAR

In ICU, one nurse looks after two patients, but in the ward one nurse looks after several rooms of four patients each. The overworked nurses couldn't spare Ken the extra time he needed. Keeping him company had been my main motivation to visit.

Now, in the ward, my presence was a necessity to keep him comfortable. Ken couldn't reposition himself in bed, so he needed assistance to roll over or adjust the pillow between his knees. By the time I arrived, his breakfast had been delivered and was sitting in front of him on a tray, stone-cold and unappetizing. Usually someone had uncovered the dish and put a utensil between his fingers, but he couldn't grip it or raise his hand to eat. I'd feed him and make sure he had enough to drink, but swallowing was difficult. He also lacked an appetite—unlike me, who enjoyed a healthy appetite and usually finished off his leftovers.

I was hoping the new room would have a better atmosphere, a more cheerful one than ICU—but it didn't. The gentleman in the bed beside Ken had just gone through eye surgery, so the window curtains were kept closed. An older gentleman, suffering from dementia, constantly made bleating noises like a sheep, day and night. The fourth occupant withdrew into himself, never speaking.

We were told that after a severe spinal cord injury, Ken should expect to be hospitalized for about one year. The majority of this time would be spent in a rehabilitation hospital, and it would likely be a one- or two-month wait for a place to become available. I found this incomprehensible. How could Ken endure such a dismal atmosphere for twelve months?

Sharon Faber

Ken had worked hard physically building solariums and had rough, calloused hands to prove it. Because he was no longer using his hands, the calluses slowly peeled away, revealing soft, supple hands I'd never seen before. This was the first characteristic of the *new* Ken I had to get used to. It was like he lost a portion of his masculinity by losing the strong, rough hands I had grown to love. This seems trivial and insignificant when you look at the big picture, but it was the first sign, the first clue, of the changes I'd be forced to deal with, not just in Ken's physical body, but in our attitudes and how we related to each other.

He still slept most of the time I was there, usually drifting off shortly after I settled into the chair beside him. I'd wake him when his lunch arrived and feed it to him, bite by bite. This was the first time I had spoon-fed an adult and I found myself chatting away, encouraging him, like I did with the kids. After he had eaten as much as he could, I'd recline his bed, get him comfortable, and within minutes he'd be sound asleep, sometimes softly snoring, his mouth hanging open. I would wake him again when the time arrived to catch my afternoon train, then kiss him goodbye with a promise to return in the morning.

A couple of hours later, Ken's evening visitors arrived to help him eat dinner. Rob's favourite game to help pass the time was a *Reader's Digest*'s quiz called "It Pays to Enrich Your Word Power," a twenty-question quiz to increase your vocabulary. Rob had stacks of old *Reader's Digests* at home and brought a new one each visit.

"What best describes the noun *chaparral*?" Rob would ask. "A shrubby habitat, a windstorm, a desert environment, or a marsh? Okay, Ken, which one do you think it is? Do you want me to read it again?"

Ken couldn't concentrate on anything, and after a few questions he would fall asleep. If he woke up, Rob continued where they'd left off. It didn't take long until the sight of Rob pulling the next *Reader's Digest* out of his back pocket sent Ken immediately into a deep sleep. This was the effect Rob had been looking for. Sleep helped his body to heal, but it also provided an escape from the constant throbbing pain.

Rob found it difficult to see his older brother so helpless. One evening, Rob and Alex sat with Ken, who was dozing in bed. Suddenly they smelled something bad. They both looked at each other, communicating their horror with their eyes. They quickly rang the nurse, but no one was around. They desperately tried again, then stood in the hall looking first one way and then the other in vain. Still no nurse came. They thought this may develop into a serious situation, that complications could arise, maybe bedsores.

Rob was aghast. *Oh no. We may have to change our brother's diaper!*

While they were trying to figure out what to do, an angel of mercy arrived dressed in white with comfy shoes. As she drew the curtain around the bed, Rob and Alex remarked to each other how much they didn't want to do it. Then they heard Ken say, from behind the curtain, "I don't blame you."

He hadn't been asleep after all!

Ken casually mentioned to his friend, Scott, that since his injury he had trouble concentrating, which hindered him from reading his Bible. Scott returned an hour later, having purchased a set of cassettes tapes which contained a dramatized recording of the entire Bible. Ken could listen to the story of Gideon defeating his enemies, Daniel in the lion's den, Jesus healing lame beggars, and Paul's inspiring letters. These treasured recordings filled countless hours of Ken's time and were an immense source of encouragement. Years later, when we went on road trips with the boys, these same tapes came along for the ride.

I wanted to see the surgeon to get an update on Ken's progress. Because Ken wasn't the type to ask questions, he wasn't a good source of information for me. Dr. Fehlings usually reviewed Ken's chart early in the morning, well before I arrived, but one morning he popped in later than usual. As he hadn't been expected, he caught me off-guard and I made the mistake of asking him, in front of Ken, what the likelihood was of Ken getting the use of his legs back. Once the question was asked, I wished I could retract it. I should have asked him privately, but it was too late now.

He paused, considered for a moment, then told us that Ken had a very low percent chance, maybe five percent, of recovering any movement in his legs, and no chance of that movement being useful to him.

I appreciated that he took the time to answer my question and was straightforward with us, but this wasn't the news I had hoped and prayed for—it was a confirmation of what I feared.

However, this news was even more shocking to Ken. This moment, the one I had been trying to protect him from, was when he first became aware that he wasn't going to walk out of the hospital. Up to this point, Ken was aware he had broken his neck, but he'd thought that when the bones healed he'd be back on his feet. He hadn't been aware that his paralysis could be permanent. I wasn't able to shield him from the truth any longer, and I knew he was upset.

Ken had a dark night. He spent hours venting to God and grieving for everything he had lost. He said goodbye to picking up his wife and spinning with her in his arms, to running with his sons and throwing them up in the air, to body-checking Rob into the boards while playing hockey. He said goodbye to a dented snowmobile filled with memories, his scuffed hockey skates, a pair of skis and ski boots which could tell stories, his worn-out work boots, the tool belt that fit just right, and his old pickup truck that he loved like a dear friend.

Ken thought the ability to think and talk was all he had left. Because he couldn't work in construction anymore, he thought all that remained was to enrol in university and become an intellectual, like Stephen Hawking, and spend his time debating the reality of creation.

As the sun started to rise in that dim, depressing hospital room, Ken realized he didn't have to say goodbye to everything. There was still one possession he had left, something he treasured more than anything else: his gift of salvation.

Along with this realization came unexplainable comfort and joy. Hope bubbled up within him. He asked himself, what did the surgeon know anyway? He wasn't in control—God was! Ken's stubbornness—or as he preferred to call it, determination—kicked in. With God's help, he decided to get back ninety-five percent movement and then the five percent lacking wouldn't matter.

Ken's faith that he'd one day run and play hockey never wavered again.

One day on my way home after spending a long day with Ken, I got off the subway and walked, with feet dragging, to the Bloor station to wait for the next train home. The station was completely empty. I walked past several hot benches in the glaring sun, choosing a cooler one situated in the shadow of an apartment building. Setting my knapsack down on the concrete platform, I plopped down on the hard bench, more tired than I had ever been before.

I couldn't get used to seeing Ken so helpless—in fact, it was getting harder. I was discouraged. Grasping what had happened to our family was impossible. It was like I stood two feet in front of a full-sized billboard with my neck craned back, trying to see what was pictured there. But no matter which way I looked, the billboard filled my vision and I couldn't make sense of it. It was impossible to step back to get a better view.

People would often comment that I was a strong woman, that I was handling Ken's situation well. This always surprised me, because I didn't feel strong but weak and frail, like a coward. I was just resting back in the peace God had given me, trying to leave the future in God's hands.

The Apostle Paul learned this lesson and tells about it in 2 Corinthians 12:9: *"But he said to me, 'My grace is sufficient for you, for my power is made perfect in weakness.'"* He goes on to say that when we are weak, Christ's power makes us strong. I wasn't the strong one; people were seeing God's strength in me.

Even though I wasn't striving to cope in my own strength, I found it more difficult to get through each day. Something was wrong. If I was to rely on Christ's strength, and I was honestly trying to do just that, why was I slowly sinking further into despair? Why wasn't Christ's strength lifting me up?

I was close to my breaking point. I couldn't carry on much longer like I had been. Something had to change.

A lady came into the station, walked past the same three or four benches I had passed, and sat beside me in the shade, also looking for relief from the heat. She crossed her legs, plopped her large handbag on her knee, and sat quietly, resting, looking off into the distance. On the

---

edge of her purse she had attached a key fob which read, "I can do all things through Christ." I recognized the scripture from Philippians 4:13 and knew that the other side of the fob read, "who strengthens me."

I stood up and walked along the platform, reciting the memory verse Mom had taught me when I was a child. I knew that God had provided this source of encouragement for me, but the verse failed to bring me comfort, even while saying it over and over. I had been trying to do all things through Christ, but where was His strength? He had promised He would strengthen me, but I felt so weak, so alone. I hardly had the strength to stand and wanted to crumple onto the concrete platform, admit defeat, and give up. I couldn't cope any longer.

My train arrived, and I rode home in a fog of doubt and confusion.

As soon as the babysitter had closed the door behind her, I phoned Linda. I didn't say much, but she knew by the sound of my voice that I had hit rock bottom. She dropped everything, drove over, prepared dinner, and bathed James and John and put them in their pyjamas. After the boys and I were settled, she went home to care for her own family.

All that remained was to read the boys their bedtime story and tuck them into bed. The story marked to be read that evening was based on Matthew 14:22–33 and entitled "Peter Gets Wet." It had several vivid accompanying pictures and went like this:

> It was night and Jesus was praying. All the people had gone home and the disciples were sailing across the lake. Can you see their boat far away?
>
> In the middle of the night Jesus decided to walk across the water to the boat. But the disciples were afraid when they saw him.
>
> "Look," they cried, "a ghost is coming!"
>
> "Don't be afraid!" said Jesus. "It's just me."
>
> Peter still wasn't sure. "If it's you, Jesus, tell me to walk on top of the water too."
>
> "Alright," said Jesus. So Peter got out of the boat.
>
> At first Peter did just fine. But when he saw the wind and the waves, he was afraid and began to sink.

"Help me, Jesus!" he cried.

Jesus reached out and caught his hand. He helped Peter get back into the boat. "Why did you look at the waves instead of me?" he asked.[6]

One picture depicted Peter, up to his knees in water, his head turned away from Jesus, with a look of horror on his face as he watched a huge wave loom up, threatening to crash over him. As I read, the last line jumped off the page: "Why did you look at the waves instead of me?" Tears rolled down my cheeks. I'd focused my eyes on my troubles instead of keeping my eyes on Jesus. I had been looking over my shoulder at the looming waves as they threatened to crash over and drown me, but Jesus wanted me to turn my head and look into His eyes. He was holding me up after all, just like He had held Peter up, and wouldn't let me sink and drown.

I learned that to lean on Jesus you have to close your eyes to your billboard of fear. Stop leaning back, trying to get a handle on your situation. Stop trying to figure it out and allow the Lord to break it down to bite-sized pieces you can handle. Then, as He leads you, just take one step.

I was trying to comprehend every implication of Ken's injury on our lives. The Lord wasn't asking me to find myself employment, to decide whether to renovate the house or move, or line up long-term childcare, all while sitting in a train station. All He asked of me was to feed my kids their dinner, ready them for bed, and get the much-needed rest I craved.

As Jesus said in Matthew 6:34, *"Therefore do not worry about tomorrow, for tomorrow will worry about itself. Each day has enough trouble of its own."* I had to learn to stop wondering what the future held. I had to let go and just follow the Lord's leading and concentrate on what today held. This is what it means to be weak. My concerns would eventually be dealt with, one by one, in God's timing. Again I was reminded to trust God and just take things one day at a time.

---

[6] L.J. Sattgast and Russ Flint, *My Very First Bible: New Testament Stories for Young Children* (Eugene, OR: Harvest House Publishers, 1989), 77–80. Used with permission.

The boys' storybook has become very special to me and is stored on my bookshelf with my other treasured volumes. Every once in a while, when I'm struggling, I take it out and look again at the picture of Peter with his horror-filled eyes as he looks over his shoulder at the threatening waves, his face turned away from Jesus.

———

Unexpectedly, Ken was scheduled to be moved earlier than anticipated from Toronto Western to Lyndhurst Hospital, a rehabilitation facility which specialized in spinal cord injuries. I had an appointment for Monday, August 23, to visit the hospital. Ken's brother Peter accompanied me. As soon as we stepped through the front doors, we were impressed. Instead of white tile floors and the smell of disinfectant, we were greeted by a large, open lobby with hardwood floors, a sitting area with couches, and a general atmosphere of warmth. Good things happened here.

A hospital representative met us, gave us a short tour of the facility, which cared for about sixty admitted patients, and explained what Ken would be doing there. He'd have a team of professionals overseeing his rehabilitation. Besides doctors and nurses, an occupational therapist would help Ken overcome the obstacles of his daily care with limited hand and arm movement. He would also have a physiotherapist to help achieve optimal mobility. Usually quadriplegics stayed about one year, as it took time to master wheelchair skills and integrate back into the community.

I was relieved to hear that Ken was scheduled to be transferred in only two days. This was to occur only two weeks after his injury. Admittance to Lyndhurst this quickly was unusual and also a blessing, because the earlier rehabilitation starts, the less time the muscles have to deteriorate. Twenty percent of muscle strength is lost for every week of paralysis.

Healing and progress could be felt in Lyndhurst's atmosphere, not sickness and disease, and I could hardly wait to tell Ken all about it.

Chapter Eight

CONQUERING PHYSIOTHERAPY

W e were both thankful for the world-class care Ken had received at Toronto Western, but we were tired of the heavy, clinical atmosphere. Ken was apprehensive about moving to Lyndhurst, so he was relieved to hear my positive report. We were ready to say goodbye to Toronto Western, to the heartbreak and turmoil we'd experienced there, and looked forward to embarking on Ken's journey of recovery. I longed to discover what our new normal would be but was doing my best to not borrow tomorrow's cares and to stay content by taking things step by step.

Ken was moved to Lyndhurst by ambulance while lying on a stretcher, because he couldn't sit upright in a chair without feeling faint. Frustrated that he couldn't see out the ambulance window, he asked his attendant for a street-by-street commentary of each turn made. He knew where Toronto Western Hospital was located, as he had driven past many times, but he wasn't familiar with Lyndhurst's neighbourhood. It bothered him that he couldn't visualize exactly where he was. After his arrival, he asked me again and again where he was, which streets I had used to get there. Finally, to settle him, I went out to the car and brought him my map book, pointing out Lyndhurst's location.

Ken's airy room held four beds and was bright with sunlight. The large window was low enough so he could look out over the parking lot while he lay in bed. The adjoining bathroom allowed a wheelchair to easily manoeuvre into it and had a roll-in shower. Every detail had been planned out carefully to accommodate wheelchairs.

None of the patients' rooms had televisions, as everyone was encouraged to leave their room to socialize and nurture new friendships. Televisions were in designated areas only, where groups of people could watch an interesting program. If someone was bedridden, one could be brought to their room to help pass the time.

Linda and Ken's brother-in-law, John, pinned up two posters on the ceiling above Ken's bed: a white one which had "I can do all things through Christ who strengthens me, Philippians 4:13" written in fancy red calligraphy, and a blue one with a white bird in flight which read "With God all things are possible, Matthew 19:26." My parents put a portrait of me, taken while we were dating, on Ken's side table, and about a week later Paul arrived for a visit carrying the skis Ken had asked him to sharpen while he was in intensive care. Paul propped them up in a corner of his room, and they stayed there until he was discharged, usually drawing a puzzled look from anyone who visited. Ken's fellow patients often referred to him as "the guy with the skis in his room." We all wanted to motivate Ken towards recovery and for him to feel at home.

Rubbing Ken's back, trying to relieve his pain, my fingers encountered bones where muscles used to be. I knew he had been losing weight but was shocked to become aware of exactly how much he had lost. Lying on his side, his hip bones stuck out unnaturally and his muscular legs, built up from years of climbing ladders and skiing, had shrunk to spindly, skin-covered bones. His body was trimmed down to almost nothing, a mere shadow of his former self. Never before had I seen him so thin, so emaciated. My first instinct was to panic, but I took myself in hand, tried to keep my concern from Ken, and instead encouraged him to finish all his meals, offering him second helpings of dessert.

Before Ken could start physiotherapy, he had to get accustomed to sitting in a chair. Ken could manage sitting up in bed, but he'd become lightheaded and pass out when his orderly moved him to the edge and his legs were lowered. This is called postural hypotension, which occurs when the body "forgets" to increase the heartrate to accommodate lower blood pressure after changing position. Sometimes if you stand up too quickly, you can have the same sensation but to a far lesser degree. Lyndhurst's nurses and orderlies were experts in dealing with this condition and in helping the body to relearn and adjust back to normal. Ken's legs were lowered off the bed and his upper body slowly moved to a sitting position. When he felt lightheaded and fainted, his upper body was lowered slightly backward until he felt better. Then the process was repeated again. By administering drugs to increase his heartrate and giving him sugary drinks, they had him over the worst part and into his motorized wheelchair in about thirty minutes. The first time he lost consciousness several times, but they assured him it would be easier next time.

Once into his motorized wheelchair, the nurse gave Ken a quick lesson on how to use the joystick, and then he took off out the door and down the hall. He was like a caged bird stretching his wings and flying free, leaving me to jog along behind. Ken could manage to stay up for only an hour the first time, but each day his tolerance slowly increased until he could stay up for several hours at a time, eventually staying in his chair all day.

The first time I watched Ken being moved to his wheelchair brought a disturbing revelation. Prior to this, I had only seen him in bed, lying on his back or with the bed slightly raised to help him eat. When his orderlies sat him completely upright, if they didn't hold him by the shoulders he'd have flopped over onto the floor. I knew that Ken couldn't move his arms and legs, but I hadn't realized that his abdominal muscles would also be useless. He proved to be even more helpless than I'd originally thought and required a wide belt around his chest to keep him in his wheelchair.

Ken's days settled into a regular routine of physiotherapy appointments interspersed with mealtimes in the cafeteria. With Ken's natural ability to chat, it wasn't long until he had made friends with everyone and was seldom found in his room. Lyndhurst offered Ken a chance to be social to his heart's desire, and he loved it. Being with others energized Ken. Every spare moment was spent talking to his fellow patients and getting to know them. His nurses struggled to keep track of where he was, regularly paging him over the hospital intercom system to return to his nursing station so they could administer his medication as scheduled.

They were also constantly tightening his neck brace. It was supposed to be worn very tight, supporting the weight of Ken's head off his neck, but he complained that it was uncomfortable worn that way and loosened it when nobody was looking. Sometimes when I arrived to visit, it looked like he was wearing a necklace around his neck and I also got into the habit of tightening it back up. While Ken was at Toronto Western, a salesman had recommended that Ken pay extra to upgrade his neck brace from the standard model to a more comfortable one. I'm glad we purchased the upgraded model, as Ken probably would have refused to wear the less comfortable model altogether.

Assisting Ken each day was no longer a priority for me as Lyndhurst had plenty of staff and volunteers available to help him. This enabled me to focus once again on running the household. Because Lyndhurst was a rehabilitation hospital, I had no qualms about bringing the boys to visit their dad and brought them whenever I could. I'd park the car, help James out, unbuckle John from his car seat, and while holding their hands tightly we would walk through the parking lot. It was like keeping eager horses reined in. Once on the sidewalk, I'd let them go and they'd run to the entrance as fast as they could. When the automatic sliding doors opened before them, they'd turn right at the reception desk and gallop down the hall to Ken's room to prance around his wheelchair, excitedly telling their latest news. My two blond-headed boys were laughing and happy to be with their dad once again. I didn't have the heart to hold them back and tell them not to run in the halls. They probably wouldn't have listened anyway.

Ken always had something new to show them or we'd walk outside along the paved pathways through the garden. Ken slowly rode along, with a small boy walking on either side holding onto the arms of his wheelchair. It reminded me of how, just a few weeks earlier, they had walked on either side of Ken's wheelbarrow, holding on and thinking they were helping.

James and John quickly won the hearts of the staff and Ken's fellow patients. Everyone loved to see their joyous, innocent faces and no one ever complained about them running down the halls.

Life at Lyndhurst, as compared to Toronto Western, was quite different because you were encouraged to take responsibility for your own care. Physiotherapists provided a customized cuff, so Ken could hold a utensil in the palm of his hand, and a guard to stop food from being pushed off his plate. Ken could now begin feeding himself.

The cafeteria was a large room with windows overlooking the garden, but it held very few chairs and had extra high tables to accommodate wheelchair armrests. Along with ordering from the menu, you'd also specify if your food should be cut or uncut, and a volunteer was provided to patients who needed assistance eating. Ken did his best to feed himself breakfast and lunch. But usually, after doing his occupational therapy all afternoon, he was tired and required a volunteer's assistance for dinner. Several weeks passed before Ken's left hand strengthened enough so he could grip the utensil himself, no longer requiring a cuff and a volunteer. He couldn't use his dominant right hand because his arm was still in a cast.

Families gathered in the cafeteria in the evenings to visit and patients gathered to play games or cards. A card game was always in progress at the table by the door, and quadriplegics used special racks to organize their cards. Someone with a broken back and full use of their arms never complained or showed frustration but waited patiently for a quadriplegic dealer to painstakingly deal out each card one by one.

Everyone at Lyndhurst had their own unique story of how they had been injured: diving into shallow water, falling backwards out of a window while cleaning it, tumbling out of a hammock, being hit by a train, or falling off a bicycle. The person who had been hit by a train walked out of Lyndhurst using only a cane for assistance and the person who had fallen out of a hammock was completely paralyzed from the shoulders down. Others suffered from blood clots, tumours on the spine, car accident injuries, or gunshot wounds.

Lyndhurst had a policy they adhered to and encouraged the family of an injured person to employ. Once a patient learned a new skill and could do something for themselves, they were to continue doing it un-assisted, even if it was awkward for them or took longer to complete. If someone was to step in unasked and assist them to put on a coat or cut their food, they'd lose the sense of accomplishment of a task conquered by themselves. In the months to come, some people criticized me for following this policy as they thought I should do everything for Ken, even when he was able to—and wanted to—do it for himself.

Once Ken's hands could grasp, a trapeze bar appeared over his bed so he could turn himself over at night. He was also given a transfer board, a long, thin, and polished wooden board used to move someone from a bed to a wheelchair. Ken was helped into a sitting position on the edge of the bed. His transfer board was then laid down from Ken's hip to the wheelchair seat like a bridge onto which an orderly helped him slide across.

Toileting routines were a popular topic of conversation among Ken's new friends. These guys hadn't thought about this function since they were three years old and now had the fun of learning it all over again. After a spinal cord injury, the body's sensations feel new and differ-ent and have to be relearned. It usually takes new patients several months to decipher them, and those who are able to feel them are considered very fortunate. Everyone learned quickly, when detecting an unexpected surprise, to laugh it off and not take accidents too seriously. We would forget that others may not be as comfortable about this as we were.

Once when Ken and I were visiting with Paul, we heard a loud, air-escaping sound. It obviously had come from Ken and we all turned towards him. He gave a small smile and, in a sheepish voice said, "Ahem. Excuse me." Ken and I immediately burst out laughing, seeing the un-comfortable look on Paul's face. We had long lost our squeamishness about such things and Paul was caught off-guard, unsure whether he should join in the laughter.

The physiotherapy room was filled with equipment: large mats where patients could be stretched and moved, treadmills for those who could walk, hand-operated stationary bikes for those who couldn't, and weights and dumbbells. There were racks with harnesses where a patient could be hoisted to a standing position, and also parallel bars to practice walking. When I visited the room, it was hard to watch other patients using the treadmills and parallel bars without feeling envious. Inside I was hoping and praying that one day Ken would use this equipment.

During one of Ken's sessions, while he was lying on a mat, his physiotherapist taught me how to stretch out Ken's legs, as I would eventually do this once or twice per day for him when he came home. His muscles were stiff and tight from being immobile for weeks and stretching them was uncomfortable, even painful. I didn't realize how heavy a human leg was to pick up, especially when it's paralyzed. I'm not sure who received the better workout—him or me. While Ken lay on the floor, his legs were lifted one at a time. I asked him to tell me when I'd raised his leg to the point where we maximized the stretch but stayed within the range of being bearable. To Ken, saying he'd reached that point was like admitting defeat, so I monitored the expression on his face instead. When he started to grimace in pain and hold his breath, I'd know it was time to stop raising his leg.

I'm afraid I didn't have much patience for this and Ken said I'd make a lousy physiotherapist.

The hospital had enticements to stay active everywhere. The garden had paved walkways encouraging a stroll (or wheel), a pool table and foosball table in the hall, and a gym. Ex-patients used the gym in the evenings to play wheelchair basketball. Ken loved to watch on the sidelines, his eyes lit up and a wide grin spread across his face. I knew he itched to hold a basketball once again, and now he hoped it would be possible.

The gym was also used to teach patients how to manoeuvre their wheelchairs. A curb-height platform had been built on which patients could practice going up and down. The patient leaned back in his chair to lift the front wheels, placed them on the platform, then leaned forward, using his arm muscles to move the back wheels against the step and wheel them up. He then turned and practiced sending the chair over the edge quickly, all four wheels landing at the same time, causing a loud thump. A physiotherapist always stood behind, ready to intercede, while beginners were first learning.

Ken's physiotherapists were waiting for the removal of the cast on his arm at the end of September so he could use a manual wheelchair. He had recovered enough movement in his arms that, as long as they could be strengthened, a power chair might not be needed. This was good news for me, because a heavy power chair would require an expensive van equipped with ramps to transport Ken.

In the afternoons, Ken went to occupational therapy to develop fine motor skills, learn how to care for himself, and assisted with integrating him back into the community. At the beginning of each session, Ken's hands and wrists were put into warm wax and then massaged and stretched until limber. Patients learned how to use their hands again by moving small objects from one dish to another and stacking blocks into a tower. Or two patients would play checkers together. Ken also used a handheld, gripper-type contraption with one elastic band on it. I was present when Ken, after days of hard work, finally managed to squeeze the gripper shut by extending the elastic band. He thought once he succeeded that he'd be finished with the silly thing and could move to something else, but he was disappointed when his physiotherapist added a second elastic and handed it back.

Ken also had a clear plastic box with a tube to blow into, which caused a small ball to rise, strengthening his chest and lungs. He'd huff and puff until he was red in the face. The best he could do was make the ball wobble back and forth. One day, after he was fed up with it, he handed it to me and said, "This stupid thing is broken." I inhaled and blew into the tube, sending the ball rocketing to the top with a clatter. Without saying a word, I just passed it back.

I remember the day I learned about nerve damage. The therapist blindfolded Ken, then placed familiar, well-known objects into the palm of his hand to feel and identify. It shocked me when Ken couldn't distinguish between a penny, button, or thumb tack. When the therapist put a screw into Ken's hand, I figured he'd recognize it for sure, because hadn't he handled those every day? When he sat silently, with a confused look on his face, it was hard for me to stay quiet and not blurt out the answer. I learned that, besides the nerves carrying messages from the brain to the muscle, nerves also carry messages back to the brain. These messages communicate temperature, soft or sharp sensations, and other details so the brain can decipher the information and know what is held in the hand.

Later, when Ken put items into his pocket, he had no idea what it contained by feeling them, so he had to carry his car keys around his neck on a lanyard. This saved us hours of time we spent searching for lost keys which had been hidden in Ken's pocket all along.

We all experience the common sensation of knowing where our bodies are without looking at them, like knowing if your arm is extended or beside your body. This sensation is vital to driving a car so you can distinguish where your feet are.

A person with a spinal cord injury can be "complete" or "incomplete." When the spinal cord is severely damaged or severed and no messages travel past the injured area, this is called complete and results in total paralysis below the injured level. Or you can have partial damage, where some messages get past the damaged area, and this is called incomplete. Because Ken had sensation and movement below his level of injury, he was considered an incomplete quadriplegic.

Rob Hurts Ken

Whenever I had business in the vicinity of Lyndhurst, I'd drop in to visit Ken. His physiotherapists didn't seem to mind me stopping by, and I wanted Ken to know I was thinking of him—that he hadn't been forgotten.

Knowing how much Ken missed being at home, I don't know how he coped with the prospect of being in the hospital so long. Only home has that special feeling. You notice it returning from vacation after you've been away.

I spent only one night in the hospital years ago after a routine procedure and hated every minute of it. My only thought was to escape that dreadful place as fast as I could. Now Ken was confined to a hospital week in and week out, probably for months. Visiting often was the only way I knew to make things easier for him.

Ken had always been a tough guy and could take a hard hit. In hockey, because we were brothers, we'd body-check each other harder than we'd dare hit anyone else. Ken would drop his head, shoot the puck, look up, and I'd clobber him real hard. I knew I'd checked him hard but he wouldn't even flinch, just get back up, grab his stick off the ice, and skate away, pretending nothing had happened. He refused to show his pain; he was tough as nails. But physiotherapy was tough on Ken. A therapist stretched out the muscles in his arms and legs each day, pushing him to the edge of his endurance. I could see that it was painful for him, but he wouldn't let it show.

This same stubbornness and toughness came out in physiotherapy, and I soon realized this would be Ken's greatest asset in the long road ahead.

When Ken was trying to get used to sitting up again, and kept passing out, he told me that it was the most difficult obstacle he had to face each day, causing him to dread getting up in the morning. He was determined to handle everything the physiotherapist threw at him, to not complain or show his pain, but instead he desired to exceed their expectations.

One evening, I was visiting Ken along with his friend, Dave. Ken sat in his wheelchair, Dave sat on Ken's bed, and I sat in a spare manual wheelchair that had been left nearby. If I could, I always chose to sit in a wheelchair when I visited Ken; some people seemed embarrassed and afraid of the chair, treating it like a bad disease to be avoided at all cost, but I wanted to try on Ken's shoes, so to speak, to understand and taste for myself some of what he was experiencing. We were chatting away and I was leaning back in my wheelchair, trying to do a wheelie like I'd watched the experienced guys do by balancing my weight on the back wheels with the front wheels raised. I was starting to get the hang of it and wasn't doing too bad, but then I got careless, lost my balance, and the front wheel of my chair accidentally came down on Ken's toe—hard.

Ken grimaced from the pain. "Owww! You jerk, you crushed my toe."

Boy, was he mad! I started to apologize, but then Dave and I looked at each other and broke into large grins.

"You can feel pain in your foot?" I asked.

"Of course I can. I think you broke it!"

"Ken, think about it. You have feeling in your foot. You should be thanking me. This is a miracle!"

"After you bash my foot, you think I should thank you? How about I clobber you!"

With Ken never admitting to pain, I knew it was excruciating, but this seemed to be good news, and I felt Ken should be rejoicing. Things were changing neurologically—something was happening! I was really sorry I'd hurt him, but also very happy. Ken, unfortunately, had trouble seeing the bright side.

This was a first on two accounts. It was the first time Ken had feeling in either of his legs, but also the first time I experienced a glimmer of hope that Ken could progress beyond his present state of crippling paralysis. I had secretly feared that Ken would remain a talking head and that, without the use of the rest of his body, leading anything resembling a normal life would be impossible.

My shoulders had carried a heavy weight fearing the future Ken had to endure, but that day I felt the worry lift, like the sun momentarily breaking through dark, stormy clouds. Perhaps it was in God's plan to heal Ken after all. I believe, if God chose, He had the power to heal him instantly, but I personally hadn't thought healing was in Ken's future.

Suddenly, his future didn't look so bleak to me. Even though he was too busy complaining about his sore toe to notice.

Chapter Nine

A BREAKTHROUGH

As Ken travelled down the road of physiotherapy and recovery, I was embarking on a journey of my own—a battle waged in my mind. I had a choice: succumb to the enemy's temptation to sink helplessly under the heavy weight of worry or fight the battle to gain victory over my peace of mind.

At odd moments, worries about the future washed over me in an instant, taking my breath away. This happened unexpectedly when my hands were wet with soapy dishwater, unable to brush away the tears running down my cheeks; while driving the car with the boys strapped in their car seats and the trunk full of groceries; or early in the morning, before I got out of bed.

Without warning, I found myself riding a rollercoaster of unanswerable questions. Could Ken work again? If so, doing what? How would I have the energy to look after young children *and* a disabled husband? How would I pay the bills? Would we have to sell our house? Would Ken be able to drive?

These were still early days in Ken's recovery and the doctors predicted that we wouldn't know the extent of Ken's permanent injuries for three to six months, or even a year. But how could I deal with these fears right now?

I couldn't waste my energy on speculation—I needed every precious ounce to deal with the present. My dilemma needed divine intervention, so I prayed for God to show me what to do. The answer returned loud and clear: sing praises to God. 2 Chronicles 20:21 says,

After consulting the people, Jehoshaphat appointed men to sing to the Lord and to praise him for the splendor of his holiness as they went out at the head of the army, saying: "Give thanks to the Lord, for his love endures forever."

The singers marched before the armed men. So that's what I did.

When I found myself plunked back into the rut of worry, or when I felt sorry for myself, I made a conscious decision to step out of the rut by singing. Over and over, I reached for my well-worn praise tapes and sang along. It didn't matter that my voice was weak and wobbly or off-key; it only mattered that I was changing my thought patterns.

I found that just having music playing in the background wasn't as effective as singing out loud. The music that worked best was my older collection, where I knew the words by heart. I played everything—old favourites from my teens, Sunday school praise music the kids enjoyed, anointed Hillsong music, and hymns which had endured the test of time.

Acts 16:25–28 tells the story of Paul and Silas. They were locked in chains and in prison, then they prayed and sang songs of praise. Miraculously, there was an earthquake and their chains fell off. I experienced this same freedom when I sang my old favourites and claimed for myself the promises and scriptural truths proclaimed. I then felt the chains of worry break, setting me free. Through this victory, I confirmed that what Isaiah 54:17 says is true, that no weapon formed against you will prosper. Isaac Watts wrote in an old hymn, "Grace is my shield and Christ my song."[7]

The enemy, when confronted with this maelstrom of worship, retreated very quickly and finally gave up his attacks.

———

Since leaving Toronto Western, Ken suffered with fevers off and on. Sometimes they were quite high, usually peaking in the middle of the night. Ken's nurses soaked towels in cold water and wrapped them around

---

[7]   Isaac Watts, "Let Me But Hear My Savior Say," 1835.

him until his fever broke. Afterward he couldn't get warm again and spent the remainder of the night huddled under his blankets, shivering.

Tests checking for an infection in his bladder and kidneys were negative. The fevers were a mystery, until one day the skin around his cast was hot to the touch and looked red and irritated. The nurses wanted to keep it elevated but weren't sure how to accomplish this because he couldn't wear a sling around his neck. A solution was found by attaching an IV pole to the side of his wheelchair and hooking his sling over it.

While cruising down the hospital halls, Ken was quite a humorous sight, which caused fellow patients to take a second look. His right arm was permanently bent at a right angle, encased in a blood-red cast and tied over his head to the IV pole. To ensure he didn't fall out of his chair, a twelve-inch-wide strap was wrapped around his chest and the back of the wheelchair. When riding over rough ground or making sudden movements, his knees knocked together and his arm swung overhead. To stop the knocking together of his knees, a piece of white Styrofoam was wedged between them, but there was no way to prevent his arm from swinging back and forth like a pendulum. To cap it off, because of the fevers, his nurses insisted he balance an ice pack on his head with a baseball hat pulled over to keep it in place. At Lyndhurst, vanity took second place to a patient's care.

In reading over my journal, I came across an old entry and have copied it here. This was written on Thursday, September 9, less than thirty days after Ken's injury. When I wrote it, I didn't know that my faith would be tested the very next day.

After Ken's accident I had to struggle with lots of ugly, black words. Some of those words were: brain damage, pain, operate, paralyzed, quadriplegic—even death. But praise God, I have also come to know the true meaning of very vibrant, colourful words: peace, friendship, hope, strength, praise, healing, comfort, glory, and love.

I have had so many people say to me, "You are handling this so well." This was not done in my own strength but God's. He has given me the courage needed to face each day.

I give all glory to Him. I can feel all the prayers of family and friends, and the people at church, and I float through each day on other people's prayers. I don't know what I would have done without them.

Sometimes it feels like I am standing in front of a mountain that I need to climb and that it will overwhelm me. But I have learned that if we trust Jesus and lean on Him, He will help us to take just one step. As time goes on and we look behind us, we can see how far we have come and how He has helped us along.

I am not over my mountain yet. I have a long way to go. But I can look back and see that Jesus has helped me every step of the way. He has never left Ken or myself for even one minute. We have felt His presence continually.

When it comes time for me to pray, I have to confess here that I find it very difficult. I have trouble bringing my requests before God, because instead I am overcome by His goodness and greatness. I always end up thanking Him for all my blessings and praising Him. The scripture *"My grace is sufficient for you"* (2 Corinthians 12:9) has new meaning for me and is very real. Habakkuk 3:17–19 says, *"Though the fig tree does not bud and there are no grapes on the vines, though the olive crop fails and the fields produce no food, though there are no sheep in the pen and no cattle in the stalls, yet I will rejoice in the Lord, I will be joyful in God my Savior. The Sovereign Lord is my strength; he makes my feet like the feet of a deer, he enables me to tread on the heights."*

———

On Friday, September 10, pus started coming out of the cast on Ken's arm, causing him to be rushed back to Toronto Western by ambulance. As Lyndhurst was a rehabilitation hospital, they didn't provide this type of care. This was a giant leap backward in his progress and we were both disappointed. Years later, Ken told me that he wept when he found out he had to return. He had been busy working at his therapy, cruising around the hospital in his wheelchair and making new friends. Back at Toronto Western, his days were once again filled with boredom, with nothing to take his mind off his pain. It also meant returning to the dismal atmosphere he hated.

I dropped the kids off at their grandparents to spend the night and met Ken at the Emergency Department to keep him company while he waited. Our suspicions were confirmed when the doctor said that Ken's elbow was badly infected and that he'd be admitted. We then settled down for a long wait until a bed became available. I had brought my Bible and read a few psalms to Ken, each of us trying to be stoic, trying to gracefully accept this bump along the road to recovery.

It was late at night, we were both tired, and I had sunk into a stupor, wishing I was home in bed. Sitting on a hard plastic chair beside Ken's stretcher, he asked, "Did you see that?"

I gave half a yawn and raised my eyebrows. "See what?"

"That."

Under the thin green sheet, he moved his right knee ever so slightly sideways, like a twitch. Instantly I was awake and alert. Since his injury, this was the first movement in his legs I had witnessed other than involuntary muscle spasms. The muscle was now tired and Ken couldn't repeat the movement when I asked him to, but my eyes had definitely seen it.

Excitement bubbled up from deep within me. I soared from the depths of discouragement to the heights of hope in an instant. This was the moment I had been longing for!

Ken then told me that he had moved it for the first time the day before. He had been discouraged and prayed to the Lord for a sign, something to confirm that everything was going to be okay, something to encourage him. The next morning, God had answered Ken's prayer and he'd moved his knee. He hadn't believed it had really happened, had been afraid to tell anyone in case he'd imagined it.

The long anticipated moment had finally arrived, and I'm ashamed to say we greeted it with disbelief.

A short while later, a bed became available and Ken would be moved to a ward in an hour or two. I decided to call it a night. We prayed together, thanking God for Ken's progress. I kissed him goodbye and then headed for home.

On the drive, I reflected on what had happened. Was God going to heal Ken? Was walking in his future? Everyone else, except Ken's medical team, had been convinced Ken would walk—at least in my presence, they spoke of it as a sure thing. But until that moment, just an hour or two ago, I had been preparing myself for the long haul of adapting to a husband with useless legs. Now, suddenly, my outlook changed. I had been unsure about the future and tried with difficulty to submit to God's will, but now I had confidence that it was God's plan to heal Ken.

Unfortunately, my timeframe wasn't quite the same as God's.

Chapter Ten

WELCOME DIVERSIONS

L inda agreed to babysit so I could, again, spend my days helping Ken at Toronto Western. He was in the orthopaedic ward in a room with three other men, on a bed beside the window.

I asked for an update every time we were together or talked on the phone. Ken was excited to update me on his progress and took great pride in showing me the new movements he could perform. There was always something. First it was his right knee moving sideways, then he could move his left knee, then he could push the top of his right foot down, then he could do it with his left foot, then he could draw up his knees. Without a doubt, this was a miracle from God. His doctor from Lyndhurst, Dr. Bugaresti, made a special visit so she could witness his progress for herself, not believing the initial report she had received.

Ken was loaned a manual wheelchair to use so he could occasionally leave his room and to prevent postural hypotension from reoccurring. While I pushed the wheelchair, Ken wheeled along his IV pole in front, allowing us to visit the atrium and courtyard for a change of scenery. Our excursions included sitting outside in the sun, along with the smokers, trying to enjoy some fresh air.

The other three patients in Ken's room were a source of considerable entertainment and a welcome diversion for us. The bed beside Ken held a senior gentleman who had recently undergone a knee operation and the anaesthetic had left him temporarily confused and disoriented. At the sound of a phone ringing, he thought it was his home doorbell and attempted to get out of bed to answer it. Even though his bedrails were raised, he was determined to climb over them to answer the door.

After a day or two, Ken learned that if the phone rang he would reassure Mr. Doorbell that everything was okay and he'd look after answering the door for him. It didn't bother Mr. Doorbell that Ken's offer of help came from someone as bedbound as he was; it calmed him down anyway.

Mr. Doorbell never complained about experiencing pain until his nurse asked him to stand up. Then, suddenly, he couldn't move a muscle anywhere in his lower body without crying out from the pain. However, late one night he managed to silently climb over the bedrail and stand up. When he tried to take a step, his knee gave way, causing him to crash to the floor, entangling him in IV lines with the pole lying on top of him, nurses running to the rescue.

The patient kitty-corner to Ken had an interesting life story. His occupation was making marionette puppets and he had once been Eaton's official puppeteer. He was also quick to tell anyone who came by that in WWII he had survived being blown up—two times.

"Once in Africa, and once in Sicily during the invasion of Italy, but that blow-up put me out of the war," he'd say.

I'd only been in the room a few hours when I had already heard the story repeated several times about his being blown up—two times.

Mr. Veteran had diabetes that caused poor circulation in his feet. One foot was very bad, and if it didn't improve quickly the foot would have to be amputated. This prospect didn't bother him at all, which seemed to indicate he couldn't comprehend everything the procedure entailed. A few days later, when it became apparent that surgery was imminent, a clipboard-bearing nurse arrived, prepared to ask the usual slew of questions. Predictably, she was regaled with the familiar story of being blown up—two times. After several minutes, she interrupted Mr. Veteran to return his attention to the questionnaire.

"Have you ever had problems with your hearing?" she asked.

"No. My hearing has always been excellent."

"Have you ever had problems with your eyes, like cataracts?"

"No. I've had a Chevrolet and a Ford, but I've never driven a Cadillac. Did you know I have been blown up—two times?"

The nurse, shaking her head, laughed and gave up. She left the rest of the questions unanswered.

The last person in Ken's room was an energetic Jamaican man with sleeping problems who lay awake all night. He received and made phone calls at all hours of the night, which added to poor Mr. Doorbell's distress. A bicycle accident had resulted in a severely broken leg just below the knee and he had undergone surgery to correct it. He sported an external fixator, a traction device that would be removed once the bone healed. Steel rods ran on either side of his leg, with pins protruding into the skin at his knee and ankle, resulting in a gruesome sight. But he insisted on exhibiting it to anyone who visited. He became quite adept at flinging back his blanket to reveal his leg, all in one quick motion. He was a busybody, demanding to know what we were doing, what we talked about, what we were reading, who was on the phone, and even what we were eating.

Mr. Busybody felt it was his duty to enlighten Mr. Veteran on exactly what the amputation entailed and to not allow this mutilation at any cost. When the nurse came to have Mr. Veteran sign the consent form, Mr. Busybody yelled, in his Jamaican accent, "Hey man. Don't let them do it!" Mr. Veteran wasn't fazed at all and calmly signed the form while replying that he would survive this as he'd survived being blown up—two times.

To help Ken pass the time, we played Battleship. As we took turns calling out coordinates and replying either "hit" or "miss," we sensed Mr. Busybody's curiosity increasing. Drawing himself up straighter in his bed, neck craned to see, he eventually couldn't keep quiet any longer and demanded to know what we were up to. He must have thought we were part of an espionage spy ring involved in blowing up battleships from the safety of Ken's hospital bed.

Observing the hijinks of Ken's roommates was a welcome change to the distressing weeks we'd just been through, and our senses of humour revealed themselves once again. With Mr. Busybody's phone ringing constantly, causing Mr. Doorbell's urgent need to answer the door, and Mr. Veteran's tall tales, we felt the Lord had provided a three-ring circus to entertain us. Our eyes kept meeting, we'd exchange a look, and then work hard to keep straight faces. Sometimes I couldn't manage it, so I'd jump up and quickly exit into the hallway before erupting into laughter. Ken didn't have this luxury and had to swallow hard, or cough lightly, in an attempt to disguise his mirth.

Ken was at Toronto Western for about ten days until the infection cleared and he was able to return to Lyndhurst—this time sitting up in the ambulance and excited to show off his miraculous progress.

Chapter Eleven

STRUGGLING TO COPE

Returning through the doors of Lyndhurst felt like a homecoming for both of us. Once more, Ken left behind the clinical atmosphere of the hospital and immersed himself in rehabilitation.

The level of Ken's pain had started to diminish, or at least his awareness of it had. Lyndhurst suggested that their patients, if possible, deal with pain without taking pain medication. Their theory was that the medication gradually wears off every few hours so you find yourself on an ever-changing teeter-totter ride of pain. Instead, if pain is left untreated the brain will eventually adapt and, over time, ignore the pain signals.

This system worked well for Ken, and after a few months his consciousness of the pain began to recede. Keeping busy also seemed to help. One day he asked me to stop inquiring about his level of pain because this caused it to be brought to his attention instead of staying in his subconscious. Of course, this method of pain management may not be appropriate for everyone.

I was also encountering, and adjusting to, unexpected situations. For years I had attended a ladies' Thursday morning Bible study which provided childcare. The fall session started in mid-September and I decided to attend in an effort to return to a regular routine, even though the thought of going made me uneasy. My whole life had been turned upside-down, I felt like a different person and didn't know if I'd fit in anymore.

In the parking lot, a dear friend who obviously hadn't heard about Ken's injury inquired about how I had enjoyed my summer. Taken by surprise, I didn't know what to say and blurted out that my husband had fallen off a ladder and broken his neck. This caught my poor friend completely off-guard, leaving her speechless and embarrassed. I still had to learn how to refer to Ken's injury with tact so others didn't feel uncomfortable.

———

The Recreational Therapy Department at Lyndhurst recommended that Ken and I plan an outing together outside the sheltered environment of the hospital to begin our integration back into the community. Ken suggested we visit a dinosaur exhibit at Ontario Place he had seen advertised in the newspaper. Neither of us was overly interested in seeing the exhibit, but it was a convenient destination. We'd be picked up at Lyndhurst by Wheel-Trans and returned three hours later. I felt like the skipper and his crew on *Gilligan's Island* setting out for a three-hour tour. We weren't the Mr. and Mrs. Thurston Howell III types but instead resembled Gilligan and Mary Ann.

The day dawned sunny and warm, perfect for our outing. The bus arrived on time, lowered a ramp, and Ken drove his power chair inside. Then the friendly driver took a few minutes to strap down Ken's chair and ensure that Ken himself was safely belted in. The driver couldn't know how monumental our trip was—like a baby's first shaky steps on wobbly legs. At the back were a few empty seats where I could sit. Stopping along the way, we let other passengers on or off, each time pausing to add or remove safety straps.

Sitting in the back of the bus on a hard seat with my purse on my lap, I felt unnatural. I couldn't act nonchalant and look out the window. Instead I was compelled to study this new version of Ken I'd never seen before, sitting just in front of me. Away from the hospital, doing something ordinary, he looked like a stranger. With unseeing eyes, he gazed awkwardly out the window. Over the last few weeks I had yearned for "normal," but this wasn't anything close to normal. I felt uncomfortable and didn't like it.

Once off the bus, the types of obstacles we'd be facing quickly became apparent. Back at the hospital we had been exposed to an environment where barriers were almost non-existent, with the needs of wheelchair users prioritized over those of the able-bodied. But after stepping off the bus, a curb sat mocking us. A rudimentary ramp had been cut into it, but it was still too steep for Ken's power chair because his footrest extended beyond the front wheels by several inches. With a bit of manoeuvring and shifting about, we made it up the ramp, but in the process we managed to slightly bend the footrest. I was worried until Ken reassured me it could be easily repaired. After purchasing tickets, we had to then step aside to wait for a side gate to be opened for us, because Ken couldn't use the turnstile.

A large tent housed the exhibits, with fat electrical cables snaking along the pavement. It was crowded with small children who darted in and out excitedly, wanting to see everything at once. Ken and I were mainly there for the experience and not too interested in the dinosaurs, which worked out well because, due to Ken's chair and the crowds, we couldn't get close to them anyway.

Anger slowly reared its ugly head within me, oddly resembling the Tyrannosaurus exhibit that glared down at me from its great height. I wanted to have a temper tantrum, a little hissy fit, right there. I wasn't angry at Ken, who displayed the greatest of patience; I wasn't angry at the parents who couldn't control their children; I wasn't angry at the cables which hid on the ground, jumping out constantly to trip us up; I wasn't angry at the imbecile who repeatedly stepped in front of Ken's chair—I was angry and frustrated at the whole situation I found myself in. I was digging in my heels, reluctant to accept the day's frustrations and just go with the flow. Several times I had to take myself in hand, inhale deeply, and will myself to stay calm.

After a quick perusal of the exhibit, Ken was tired and had reached the limit of his endurance. We slowly made our way back to the bus stop, well ahead of the appointed pickup time. I found a bench for me, and we decided to sit and enjoy the sunshine. We were both unnaturally quiet and wanted to return to the safe, easy atmosphere of Lyndhurst.

Our outing had been a disappointing eye-opener. We had been together the whole time, but—oddly—very much apart. I hadn't been
able to sit beside Ken on the bus, and I'd had to walk behind Ken's chair
because of the crowds. He had been sitting down while I was standing
up. I hadn't been able to hear him unless I bent down to his level. Was
this a taste of our future? Would the fun times we'd enjoyed together
ever return? I'd known our outing wouldn't be easy, that there would
be physical obstacles to overcome, and I'd thought of it as having an adventure—but I hadn't been prepared for how awkward the day turned
out to be. Like an episode of *Gilligan's Island*, everything had gone awry.

———

When the cast on Ken's arm was removed, he was promoted to a manual wheelchair. This turned a trip down the hallway to his physio appointment into a major expedition. Instead of being propelled by a
battery-operated chair with a joystick control, Ken had to rely on his
diminished muscle power. His arm muscles had deteriorated and atro-
phied, so moving just a few feet required all his strength. He had to stop
multiple times for rests along the hallways. Sometimes in the evening,
tired from a long day, I'd help him along, joking that not every husband
allows his wife to "push him around."

With Ken now using a manual chair, his medical team, much to our
delight, started working towards Ken coming home for a day visit. But
before this could happen, a couple of hurdles needed to be overcome.

Ken couldn't urinate on his own, so he was catheterized every four
hours. The hospital called it intermittent catheterization (IC). Lacking
dexterity in his hands meant he couldn't do this for himself, so his nurses
and orderlies performed his ICs for him. Ken had never imagined family
members would have to perform this intimately private task for him.

Before Lyndhurst approved a day visit, two people (a primary
and a backup) had to learn how to do Ken's ICs. I was the obvious first
choice, but who would be our backup? Much to my relief, and to Ken's

embarrassment,[8] Rob volunteered. He lived just a few minutes' drive from our house and learning to do this would allow them to enjoy outings together. I don't recall anyone asking Ken's permission. I mean, he didn't really have a say—did he? This was all for his own good. Right?

Gathered around Ken's bed along with his orderly, Rob and I rolled up our sleeves and exchanged a look that said, *Let's get this over with.* Rob and I took turns practicing, under the orderly's supervision, while Ken lay there, silently daring either of us to make a wrong move.

"Ken, you'll get over it," I couldn't help saying with a smirk and twinkle in my eye.

A part of me stepped back, viewing the situation from afar and wondering if this could really be happening.

Later, Ken and I had a good chuckle over the ridiculous sight the three of us must have made. Finally, we were laughing again. It felt so good—so normal.

At home, there were four steps to climb before reaching our front door, so the next obstacle to overcome in preparing for Ken's visit was to build a temporary ramp to enable Ken access to our main floor. It was a nice ramp, sturdily built, with slats so it wasn't too slippery. It was wide enough to accommodate Ken's chair, but to me it looked a little too steep. Maybe, with my tennis shoes on and a running start, we'd make it up. Saturday was only a few days away, so I decided to deal with the issue later.

Once inside, the rest of the house was accessible. The master bedroom and bathroom were on the main floor and the doorways were wide enough to accommodate his wheelchair. The only rooms Ken couldn't access were the boys' upstairs bedroom and the basement. Everything was coming together nicely.

Ken's day visit home was finally scheduled for Saturday, October 2. We'd been anticipating and working towards this day for the last seven weeks. Not knowing how the day would unfold made me feel excited and apprehensive at the same time, like embarking on a journey to an unknown destination.

Once again, I prayed for the Lord's help and left the details to Him.

---

[8] Ken jokingly pronounced this word as "em-*bare-ass*-ment."

Chapter Twelve

HOMECOMING

The meals had been prepared beforehand, the house was freshly cleaned, and everything was set. We were ready to welcome Ken home. The boys and I got up, ate our breakfast, and drove the now familiar route eastward on Highway 401, turning south on Bayview Avenue.

At Lyndhurst, the boys chattered away, scampering around Ken's chair, eager to head home. As we waited, Ken was given his morning blood thinner injection so he could last twelve hours away from the hospital before the next one was due.

Taking Ken's transfer board with us, we headed to the hospital's pharmacy for the medications and other paraphernalia Ken would need. The pharmacist explained when his next medications were due and handed me a large paper bag filled with bottles, tubes, and small packets, everything I'd possibly need to look after Ken at home.

Ken's orderly followed us to the car, helping Ken get settled—fastening his seatbelt, closing his door, and lifting the wheelchair into the back of the station wagon for me. He seemed a little unsure about letting us go until I told him that Rob would meet us at home.

We smiled and waved goodbye as we drove away. I felt strange to be the driver with Ken sitting in the passenger seat. He looked awkward hanging onto the overhead handle. Ken had always been my chauffeur.

Colourful balloons and streamers fluttering in the breeze caught my eye as we pulled into the driveway. Someone had tied them to our front railing to welcome Ken home, which added to the festive mood. Rob, right on time, drove in behind us and helped Ken out of the car and into his wheelchair using the transfer board. Rob eyed the steep ramp, spit onto the palms of his hands, rubbed them together, wiped his feet on the driveway to clean his shoe treads, and using all his strength pushed Ken up the ramp and onto the porch. A tense moment followed while manipulating the chair over the threshold, but then—all of a sudden—Ken was home. Rob made arrangements to return in the evening to help Ken into the car, then quickly left.

Ken spent a few minutes touring the house and I asked if he felt strange after being away so long. Did it still feel like home? He assured me that it did, that being home felt right, that nothing had changed and it almost felt like he hadn't been away at all. I was reminded again how easily we take for granted the little things in life and how quickly our lives can change.

We spent the day quietly. The boys played on the floor beside Ken, eager to show off the new skills they'd learned. Later, we shared a leisurely meal and unhurried, casual conversation around the kitchen table. These components of our lives hadn't changed, but now a transfer board waited on a chair and a row of medicine bottles lined my kitchen counter. Ken, sitting in his wheelchair, looked out of place. We were the same—but different. Ken and I had matured and grown in the last seven weeks, in ways we hadn't yet comprehended, and I felt older than twenty-nine. Our priorities had been rearranged. What had been important just a few months ago now didn't even matter.

The hours passed without a hitch, and suddenly it was time to leave.

Back at the hospital, Ken's nurses were anxious to hear how we had managed, and after hearing of our success they suggested I return the next morning for a repeat performance. Ken and I looked at each other and simultaneously agreed to their suggestion.

Since our two day visits had gone so well, Ken's medical team called a meeting to discuss when he could start coming home for the weekends. They asked me questions about the accessibility of our bathroom, the width of our bedroom door, and if I was okay with performing ICs during the night. Everyone agreed to work towards an overnight visit the very next weekend. They reassured me by saying that if anything was to go wrong, I just had to call an ambulance. Instead of reassuring me, it made me wonder exactly what could go wrong.

Rob made arrangements to modify our ramp so I could get Ken in our front door by myself. If everything went as planned, Ken would be home for Thanksgiving—an appropriate time for a homecoming gathering.

———

When the nurse asked if I was comfortable administering an injection, I didn't flinch or hesitate. I confidently said I could do it—no problem. Inside, I thought I would die. Give him a *needle!* No one had mentioned this in the meeting with Ken's team. My knees felt weak just thinking about it. Due to a frightening experience I'd had as a young child, I hated needles with a passion. Once, after receiving one, I'd even fainted. I couldn't fathom how I would do it. I fervently wished it could be quickly thrown in, like a dart.

The nurse gave me step-by-step instructions: loading the needle, measuring the medication to draw up, wiping an alcohol swab over Ken's exposed stomach, pushing the end of the needle in, and slowly pressing the plunger. Before doing it for real, she gave me a few needles to practice with at home on an unpeeled orange or raw chicken breast. For a few days in a row, I thawed chicken and injected it with water before cooking it for the kids' dinner.

Now, a dead chicken was one thing. How could I muster the courage to plunge it into the love of my life? Did I mention he was injected with a blood thinner called warfarin—rat poison? Knowing this made the experience even more stressful, but ready or not, I returned to Lyndhurst to get the first shot over with.

Hiding my fears, I managed it like a pro, keeping a calm face until the nurse had left. Afterward I sank down on a chair to catch my breath. I'd done it. We'd overcome the last obstacle, and Ken would be home for Thanksgiving.

However, I was far from confident this needle business would be a positive experience at home.

Ken hid from me that he was apprehensive about coming home overnight. He never mentioned it during his team meetings, nor told anyone, but the idea scared him. At the hospital, a team of trained professionals assisted Ken. Orderlies helped him out of bed in the morning, dressed him, performed his ICs every four hours, and helped him to bed at night. Nurses dispensed his medications at the correct time and gave him injections every twelve hours. Volunteers in the cafeteria cut his food and, if necessary, fed him. At home, just one person would be responsible for all this, but she also had the added responsibility of a four-year-old and a toddler.

I was also nervous, but I decided to tough it out and put on a brave face. The boys missed having their father at home and it had started to affect their behaviour. More than anything, I wanted our family back together—back to normal.

———

When Ken visited home for the day, I was given one large paper grocery bag filled with everything he required medically. For a weekend, I was handed *two bigger* paper bags. They contained Metamucil, a fibre that resembles birdseed to be taken each morning; Milk of Magnesia, a laxative which had to be taken three times per week; a stool softener, taken two times per day; a muscle spasm reducer, taken several times per day; antibiotics, for his recovering elbow infection; pain medication, to be taken if needed; a vial of blood thinner to prevent blood clots, to be given by injection every twelve hours; a handful of IC tubes; packets of lubricant, rubbing alcohol, and antiseptic; needles; band-aids; cotton balls; latex gloves; medicine measuring cups; and a stack of blue disposable under-pads to protect the bed when doing nightly ICs. When I lugged the loot away, I wondered if the pharmacist had anything left in his storeroom.

Rob met us at home once again to ensure that, with the modified ramp, I could manage to push Ken into the house by myself. I donned my runners, wheeled Ken a distance from the ramp so we could pick up speed to gain momentum, then hit the ramp, digging my toes in for traction. Muscles straining, I was just able to make it up the ramp and into the house. Afterward I did a victory dance, accompanied by the boys' cheers and high-fives.

Once Ken was settled, my first important task was to line up his medicine bottles and write out a schedule of when pills, ICs, and injections were needed. The list was long, but organizing it into black and white helped me feel more in control. I then set a timer for the next scheduled item, as a reminder.

Waking up the first morning, feeling Ken beside me, was heavenly. In the early morning light, I turned my head and saw Ken's profile as he lay on the pillow beside mine. My eyes grew wide with shock. I became fully awake instantly when I saw the silhouette of his wheelchair. In the fog of first waking, I had forgotten that Ken had been injured; the sight of his wheelchair brought it all back in a rush. Thankfully, Ken was still sleeping and didn't witness my confusion.

I dressed the boys when they woke and then helped Ken get up, which proved to be a workout for me. The boys' limbs were small and flexible and putting on their clothes didn't require any effort, just patience. Ken was full grown and heavier than I was. The part I hated most about dressing him was putting on his compression stockings. Ken wore tight, thick, leg-length elastic stockings to guard against blood clots. The only way I could get them on was while he lay flat on the bed. I supported his heavy leg on my shoulder and then worked them up his leg using both hands. Dressing him required all my strength, causing me to pant afterward like I'd just completed a twenty-minute workout. After Ken's stockings and pants were on, I'd swing his legs over the edge of the bed and, using his transfer board, half-lift, half-slide him into his wheelchair. I'd stand in front, with Ken holding my shoulders, and say, "Okay, on three. One, two, three." Then we'd both lift and pull together.

Everything Ken and I did had an audience of two, James and John. We made a game of counting together, but they added a long, drawn-out "Puuull" and a triumphant cheer of "Hurray!" every time Ken was moved. It made the tough tasks easier, turning a difficult chore into a fun family game.

The hospital lent us a commode chair to assist in Ken's bathroom routine while at home. Due to the size of our bathroom, we decided to transfer Ken onto the commode in the hall, then push it into the bathroom.

This seemed like a good plan in theory, but we hadn't anticipated two hitches.

First, all four wheels on the commode chair turned in all directions. Invariably, if I pushed straight ahead, it moved sideways; if I tried to turn, it moved forward. I tried standing in front, guiding it forward by pulling, but this didn't work either.

Second, our bathroom floor was half an inch higher than the hall floor due to a newer flooring installation. The transition cover over the seam had never been an issue before, but it sure was an issue now! I had to bump the front wheels over, then squeeze past Ken while he sat in the doorway and push the back wheels over, all the while each wheel trying to move in a different direction.

Ken found all this manoeuvring and bumping uncomfortable, because the urge to go was usually pretty urgent. To top it off, each move was accompanied by our audience's combined chorus of "One, two, three, puuull!" Ken didn't see the humorous side until I started laughing. Bent over, clutching my middle and howling with laughter, I was so weakened that further attempts had to wait until we'd calmed down. After the fiasco of our first attempt, Ken always hesitated slightly before mentioning that he needed to use the bathroom.

I can still see Ken as he sat in the kitchen in his wheelchair, waiting for the dreaded injection, holding his shirt up to expose his stomach. First he searched for the area with the least feeling and pointed it out, assuring me he wouldn't feel anything. His nurses alternated sides, but not when I did it—we'd always select the numbest side. Afterward we'd both breathe a big sigh of relief while he tucked in his shirt. It was the time of day I hated most.

Even more than getting injections, Ken hated swallowing Milk of Magnesia. I'd measure out the white, chalky, phlegm-like liquid into a little plastic medicine cup, then hold it out and tell him he'd get over it. His shudder afterward told it all. A few weeks later, I mentioned to his pharmacist, while Ken was with me, how much he hated taking Milk of Magnesia, only to be told quite casually that it was also available in pill form.

"Pill form!" Ken piped up. "You mean I've been choking that stuff down when I could just swallow a few pills?"

To his relief, he never took liquid Milk of Magnesia again.

Ken had the bright idea to sit on the couch. This didn't appear to be an obstacle—until he actually sat down and sank ten inches. Immediately we realized we had a problem, because I wasn't strong enough to lift him back to the wheelchair's height.

I wondered briefly if this would be considered one of the things which could go wrong only to be solved by a call for an ambulance.

It took us a few minutes to come up with a plan. Taking the seat cushion from the other end of the couch and putting it beside Ken meant I only had to lift him a few inches to the new cushion. We repeated this process until he was at the other end of the couch sitting on three cushions. The kids assisted by accompanying each move with loud, drawn-out yells of "Puuull" followed by victory cheers.

We were successful, but months passed before Ken suggested trying out the couch again.

To celebrate Ken's first weekend home, I invited our parents, along with Linda and Alex and their two children, for Thanksgiving dinner. My mom brought a cooked turkey, stuffing, gravy, and pumpkin pie. Linda brought the vegetables. Our Thanksgiving prayer was longer than usual as we thanked the Lord for all He had done for us.

Monday evening, I returned Ken to Lyndhurst. Because our first weekend had gone smoothly, with no catastrophes, Ken could now return home every weekend.

I contemplated the weekend, which in one sense had been successful as we hadn't faced any obstacles we couldn't overcome with the Lord's help. However, looking after James, John, and Ken had left me physically and emotionally drained. A good night's sleep wouldn't cure me—I was exhausted.

When the time came to return Ken to Lyndhurst, I had been secretly relieved. I'd thought Ken's recovery would be a slow incline with life getting easier, with the most difficult days behind us, but it wasn't working out that way. The brunt of the responsibility would soon settle firmly on my shoulders, because Ken was, understandably, totally absorbed in his physiotherapy and recovery. My fear grew that I wouldn't be able to cope in the weeks and months ahead.

Once again, I reminded myself to stop worrying, trust Jesus, and rest in His arms. He knew what the future held and would support me.

Chapter Thirteen

FIRST STEPS

L yndhurst had a room in the basement with a sign outside that read "Hydrotherapy." When I first noticed the sign, I had to take a second look; mental images of strange experiments using electricity filled my imagination.

I was disappointed to learn that hydrotherapy just refers to therapy in water. This chlorine-scented, echoing room contained a pool filled with warm water, and it quickly became Ken's favourite retreat. His twice weekly sessions were definitely highlights of his time at Lyndhurst. The therapist lowered a life-jacket-clad Ken into the four-foot pool using a special winch system and sling, then Ken's legs were stretched and moved in the warm water. Because the life jacket supported Ken's weight, he was finally able to stretch the kinks out of his back, and the warm water relieved some of his pain.

At the end of one particular session, Ken asked if he could try standing between the parallel bars mounted on the pool floor. Ken's therapists were realistic about his limitations and what he should attempt, but Ken wasn't so realistic and wheedled with them to comply. The therapists sometimes gave in to his requests, figuring the easier route was to allow his inevitable failure to prove the point. However, he quite frequently exceeded their expectations and both of them enjoyed the surprise of victory.

His therapist reluctantly complied this time. As they had thought, one leg wasn't strong enough to support him, but his other leg could support his weight, even if just barely, to his therapist's amazement.

About a week later—according to my journal, on Wednesday, November 3, at 10:10 a.m. while working in our office at home—the Lord impressed on me to stop what I was doing and pray for Ken. Looking at the clock, I realized that it was Ken's scheduled pool time. I immediately bowed my head and prayed, asking God to enable Ken to walk, and specifically for more control over his legs.

I knew my prayer was being answered and something good was happening. Therefore, I wasn't too surprised when Ken phoned a little later, excited and proud to tell me that he'd taken his first steps in the pool. It took all the concentration and effort he could muster, but after about ten minutes he had managed to walk ten baby steps. He even had more control over his legs, as I had prayed for. Afterward, he was left totally exhausted, but also totally convinced that the hard struggle was over, that the rest would be easy-peasy.

Little did he know that this was only a very small taste of the hard work yet to come.

Ken craved more than his twice weekly pool appointments, so Rob set aside his Saturday mornings to take Ken to our local therapeutic pool. Ken was determined to walk again and Rob figured Ken was stubborn enough to do it. With life jackets strapped to each of them, they faced each other with Rob holding the front of Ken's jacket. They floated to the deep end and then slowly moved to the shallow end. When Ken's feet could touch the bottom, he'd walk as many steps as he could before collapsing in the shallower water. They repeated this until Ken's muscles were exhausted and his legs couldn't move anymore.

After weeks of hard work, on a Saturday they will always remember, Ken triumphantly walked the length of the pool by himself.

———

The weekends were becoming less stressful for me as Ken assumed more of his own care. Enough strength had returned in his arms so that he could transfer himself with just the aid of his transfer board. The dexterity in his fingers had improved, too, enabling him to perform his own ICs, which thankfully were no longer needed during the night. A recent ultrasound showed that he wasn't susceptible to blood clots, either, so we could say goodbye to the thick compression stockings. Little by little, he was progressing.

The boys and I settled into a regular routine. On Mondays, we relaxed at home, taking it easy. On Tuesdays and Wednesdays, we drove to Lyndhurst after dinner and visited Ken. On Thursdays, we went to Bible study and purchased groceries. On Friday evenings, we returned to Lyndhurst to pick up Ken for the weekend. On Saturday mornings, Ken went to the pool, then the rest of the day was spent enjoying time together, usually at home. On Sunday evenings, we returned Ken to Lyndhurst. Like a library book, Ken was checked in and checked out regularly.

On the days I didn't visit Ken, after the boys were sleeping, we'd chat on the phone, reconnecting at the end of the day. I found it easier to cope once a regular routine was established, knowing ahead of time what each day would hold. I'm a creature of habit, thriving on knowing how a day or week will unfold—unlike Ken, who loves spontaneity and surprises.

Reading also helped me cope, so I checked out library books regularly. After I'd settled the boys for the night and chatted with Ken over the phone, curling up with a good book was therapeutic; adding a bowl of buttery popcorn made it divine. Reading was an escape that relieved my stress and helped me to fall asleep each evening.

November unfolded into a month of firsts. November 3 was Ken's first steps in the pool, and on November 7 he attended a Sunday service at our church for the first time since his injury. Everyone was happy and enjoyed seeing us. Our pastor even publicly welcomed us from the pulpit.

On November 8, Ken stood for the first time outside the pool—on dry land. His therapists helped him up, held his knees straight to keep them from bending, and while holding the parallel bars Ken stood with his legs supporting his weight.

On November 17, Ken called me with the fantastic news I'd been waiting for—his first steps! He described them as small and shaky, but it was a start. I was too excited to wait any longer to witness the event, so the boys and I made a surprise visit to watch the next day. We were just in time to see him standing straight and tall between the parallel bars, with a therapist on each side to assist. He swung his right foot out in front by thrusting his hip forward, transferred his weight, locked his knee, and then moved his hip on the other side, which propelled his left foot forward. His physiotherapists, with smiling faces, encouraged Ken at each step, gratified to see such amazing progress.

Tears filled my eyes and I had to wipe them away so I could see. I felt proud of him and overwhelmed by thankfulness to God. This was the moment we had been praying for and anticipating. For weeks I'd imagined how it would be, but when the actual moment arrived it felt surreal. Sitting in the gym on a blue floor mat, with colourful game lines painted on the shiny hardwood floor, I gathered the boys in my arms, turned them so they could watch, and explained what was happening in a voice choked with tears. I can remember the moment like it was yesterday, and the emotion I felt then still wells up within me. The Lord's presence and love surrounded me like warm sunshine, so tangible that I could have hugged it in my arms like I was holding James and John. God was faithful to answer my prayers.

Earlier, Ken's therapists had tested the individual strength of each muscle in his legs and told him that they weren't strong enough to enable him to walk—but he was doing it, leaving them speechless.

Sometimes God doesn't answer our prayers immediately but rather answers them gradually over a period of time. In Exodus 23:28–30, God knew what was best for the Israelites and delivered them slowly, little by little, giving them time to increase and take possession of the land they had been promised instead of driving their enemies out at once. Just because God does something gradually doesn't diminish the magnitude of His miracle. Ken and I knew, beyond the shadow of a doubt, that Ken's steps were a gift from God, an answer to our prayers.

———

Ken returned to Toronto Western Hospital every few weeks so his surgeon, Dr. Fehlings, could monitor his recovery and progress. Unfortunately, his interns usually saw Ken, as Dr. Fehlings, a busy individual, was frequently summoned from his regular appointments to attend to emergencies. It wasn't until the end of November that Dr. Fehlings was available to personally see Ken again. The surgeon had given Ken a zero chance of walking, so we both looked forward to demonstrating Ken's baby steps.

The doctor proceeded through the routine examination, checking reflexes, asking Ken to move his arms and grip his hands. When he finished, Ken proudly told him that he'd started walking in therapy. With great effort, Ken stood up from his wheelchair and, while holding my shoulder and the doctor's, took two small steps. This quickly tired Ken, who then flopped back down into his wheelchair.

Dr. Fehlings was speechless, sitting with his jaw dropped, leaning back in his swivel chair, disbelief and amazement written all over his face. He gathered together his interns and Ken repeated the performance for the group of young students. They were all dumbfounded. Dr. Fehlings attributed the remarkable progress to medical science and the newest innovations of treatment, but we knew it was due to prayer and God's grace.

Even if Ken was to progress to walking normally, his doctors and physiotherapists advised that earning a living in the construction field may not be possible. Climbing ladders, carrying heavy tools, and long days working outside in summer and winter could prove to be beyond his capabilities.

A government-sponsored program paid the education expenses for people to retrain in different vocations due to long-term disabilities. This program fit Ken perfectly. His building experience, coupled with his interest in drafting, pointed towards pursuing a career as an architectural designer. After Ken passed an aptitude test with flying colours, he was accepted into the program. It would pay for his education and computer expenses after he was recovered sufficiently to attend school. Obtaining basic computer skills was an urgent need, because Ken was computer illiterate and didn't know anything about them.

Lyndhurst had a classroom with a teacher who was available for high-school-aged students. Besides helping students keep up with their studies, the teacher also taught basic computer classes for interested patients. This was an invaluable opportunity for Ken, so he signed up for a beginner class on Windows and learned how to send emails. The range of computer knowledge he needed to acquire before being ready to master AutoCAD, a design and drafting computer program, was daunting, to say the least. But when someone else would have thrown up their hands in defeat, Ken just dug in and kept at it.

Chapter Fourteen

FAMILY TIME

Our eighth wedding anniversary fell on a Tuesday and I was unprepared for how difficult it would be. Ken's mom and dad came to our house to babysit so Ken and I could spend the evening together. I drove to the hospital, helped Ken into the passenger seat of our station wagon, loaded his wheelchair into the back, and climbed into the driver's seat. Then we set out without a definite destination in mind.

I had imagined a romantic dinner for two in a dimly lit restaurant, holding hands across the table. Unfortunately, we weren't familiar with the area and drove aimlessly looking for somewhere to eat as darkness slowly descended. The restaurants we drove past either had steps out front or looked sad and neglected. Nothing seemed right. Finally we settled on picking up a pizza and eating it from our laps while sitting in the car.

Our long search had altered our moods and we'd run out of things to say. Our evening had turned out to be disappointing, and oddly uncomfortable. Afterward we told each other that we'd had a nice time, pretending the evening was a memorable one—which it was, but for all the wrong reasons. We weren't very successful at hiding our disappointment and discouragement from each other.

The difference between our celebration this year as compared to prior years was startling. This was the same Ken I'd known for years, but also a brand-new Ken. He was unsure of his new limitations. His awkward wheelchair placed restrictions on him he'd never experienced before. One or two steps, even a high curb, was an insurmountable obstacle.

Sharon Faber

He had started taking his first steps, but my expectations were still too high. I wanted the old Ken back—now. If Ken was going to recover completely, which we hoped for, why was coping so hard? It slowly dawned on me that I had to learn to deal with and accept Ken's limitations, that putting in time while waiting for the end result wouldn't be enough. I had to start making an effort to know him again, like when we'd first dated.

On Friday night, Peter drove Ken home for the weekend and Ken asked him to stop along the way to purchase a dozen long-stemmed roses as a belated anniversary surprise. I buried my face in the deep red, velvety blooms, inhaled their fresh scent, and let my love for Ken wash over me. We were back on track. No matter the outcome, with God's help, we'd make it through.

———

Ken had progressed to the point where he could begin walking with the aid of a walker. His steps were still slow and he moved very carefully, but his strength was gradually returning. Christmas was only two weeks away and we hoped he could bring a walker home with him so he wouldn't regress. Our thoughts turned towards the celebration of Christmas and the prospect of being together for two whole weeks.

Linda and Alex cut a Christmas tree for us when they went for theirs and delivered it right to our door. The tree now stood in the living room, decorated with coloured balls and twinkle lights, waiting for the wrapped gifts. The menu was planned, the house sparkling clean, the gift shopping conquered, and the stockings stuffed. The to-do list was empty and everything ready, but something was missing—Ken. We counted down the days until he would be home. I wasn't too concerned about coping with Ken for such a long stretch, because he had resumed almost all of his personal care.

Christmas Day unfolded exactly as I had hoped and dreamed. The four of us opened our stockings while sitting together in our bed. Then we enjoyed a pancake breakfast, read the Christmas story, and took our time unwrapping gifts. We simply enjoyed being together while carols played softly—a quiet, peaceful day.

Boxing Day was spent celebrating with Ken's family at his parents' house, and later in the week my family joined us at our house.

Ken wasn't home too long before a slight problem arose. James quickly figured out that his dad couldn't climb stairs. If Ken wanted James to pick up a toy, or to reprimand his behaviour, James would run upstairs out of Ken's reach.

One day I walked through the living room to see Ken parked at the bottom of the stairs, waiting patiently. I had an inkling of what had occurred and asked if I should bring James down.

"No," Ken said. "He has to come down eventually."

James had no idea of the level of stubbornness—I mean, determination—he was dealing with. A four-year-old would be no match for the unmovable mountain waiting for him at the bottom of the stairs.

Within twenty to thirty minutes, James realized that Dad wasn't moving, that the only road to freedom ran past him, and he'd have to face him sooner or later. A sheepish and contrite-looking James slowly descended the stairs, one at a time. Holding the handrail above his head, which was taller than he was, he stood on the bottom step so he could look straight into his dad's eyes while he apologized. Ken had won the battle, and James never ran away from him again.

Ken tried to practice walking with his walker, but it didn't work out as well as he hoped. He was nervous about standing up, with the boys scampering about like a couple of squirrels, for fear of falling on them. Waiting until the evening when they were in bed didn't work either, because by this time Ken had tired himself out.

Concerned that he'd regressed at the end of the two weeks, he was ready to return to Lyndhurst and his physiotherapy.

With mixed feelings, I returned Ken to Lyndhurst in the new year. Part of me was saddened because I had enjoyed him being at home, but I was also having doubts about Ken returning home full-time. Having Ken home was like caring for another child. I had developed an instinct, an extra sense, about James and John's whereabouts and what they were doing, even when they were playing in a different part of the house. A part of my mind was attuned to them and making sure they stayed safe. This same awareness had developed for Ken. My ear was always listening, monitoring everything he was doing, ready to run to his rescue if he got into trouble and needed me.

I also wondered how Ken would fill his days. Would he be sitting at home all day? Would we get on one another's nerves?

Confiding my fears to Linda, she reminded me that the Lord wouldn't let me down now. She encouraged me to remember how He had been faithful over the past few months. This was the pep talk I needed, and once again I reminded myself to trust Jesus. I wondered if I'd ever learn this lesson.

You must be tired of reading about all my doubts and fears, of my treading down the same familiar path again and again. Why does it take so long to learn the lessons the Lord is trying to teach us? Instead of stepping back and being content to wait for the Lord's timing, I fought His plan for my life, wishing and longing that things had turned out differently.

In looking back, I can see that I only trusted the Lord at a surface level, relying on my own strength to get me through. I had faith that my physical needs would be met, but I didn't trust Him in the deepest part of my being as He was trying to teach me to do.

Chapter Fifteen

FREEDOM IN FEBRUARY

Two weeks without therapy hadn't hindered Ken's progress as we feared. The first week in January, he set a new record for himself by completing two laps around the gym with his walker.

One Sunday in mid-January, the Faber family gathered at Ken's parents' house for a get-together. Ken's brothers went out snowmobiling, and when they came in for a break Ken said that he wanted to try it out. It was a bright, bitterly cold day, so we bundled Ken up in multiple layers to keep him warm. I had my doubts that he'd be able to move at all after being wrapped up so tightly.

Rob strapped a helmet on Ken's head, carried him piggyback-style through the deep snow, and helped him onto the snowmobile. Everyone came out of the house to watch and stood around shivering, shouting advice and warnings for them to be careful. Rob pull-started Ken's machine, then Ken squeezed the accelerator and took off down the trail with Rob following close behind on his own machine. We all cheered, raising our arms in the air, then hurried back inside seeking the warmth of the woodstove.

Twenty minutes later, Ken returned. He stopped beside the house, turned off the snowmobile, and collapsed in the snow, lying on his back with his arms flung out to either side. Concerned that he may have hurt himself, I ran outside. Kneeling in the snow, I leaned over him, flipped open his helmet's visor, and was greeted by a giant ear-to-ear grin. He was exhausted but also jubilant, enjoying the gas-tinged scent of freedom.

One weekend, Ken came down with the flu, which made him so weak that he couldn't get out of bed. I called Lyndhurst on Monday morning, letting them know that he'd be back there in a day or two. Word soon spread and by the end of the day everyone in the building knew that Ken, a patient, had called in sick to a hospital. We didn't get the joke until Ken returned and had to endure the teasing.

Ken was steadier on his feet and progressed to walking with two canes in physiotherapy. To me, he looked a little shaky and unsteady, like a frail old lady creeping at a snail's pace, but each step brought him a few inches closer to recovery. Since he was walking with canes, his physiotherapists decided he was ready for the next step—climbing stairs. Working hard, Ken progressed to climbing a full flight, as long as each side had a sturdy handrail to grasp.

We happily ticked off this new milestone: going upstairs to tuck the boys in at bedtime. They thought this a novel idea, forgetting that it had been commonplace just six months earlier.

Getting from the floor up into his wheelchair unaided took several weeks of hard work to accomplish, as every muscle group is involved, including the core muscles. Ken found this skill the most difficult of all to achieve, even harder than walking. The accomplishment relieved his fear of falling out of his wheelchair and being unable to get back in.

———

Ken's team at Lyndhurst began discussing the subject of a discharge date. They had taught him everything they could and his remarkable progress had peaked. Because Ken had progressed so rapidly, his initial prognosis of a one-year stay had been cut in half. His discharge date was tentatively set for the end of February, but it relied on passing one more test.

A couple of rooms on the second floor of Lyndhurst were set up as an independent apartment. It even sported its own kitchen, where Ken would stay by himself for a couple of days. They did this to ensure that he could live self-sufficiently. The test also involved traveling to a grocery store, purchasing food, returning with the groceries, and preparing a hot, nutritious meal for himself. The menu had to be approved beforehand—no ordering in pizza.

This news excited Rob. "Ken, here's your chance to learn to cook! You can now help Sharon in the kitchen."

Rob knew that Ken was culinarily challenged, but he had high hopes of Ken becoming a real chef. These hopes were quickly dashed when he learned Ken had decided to make Cheese Dreams for his test dinner.

Cheese Dreams, a summer lunchtime treat I occasionally prepared, was an open-faced bun covered with processed cheese topped with pieces of hot dog and chopped tomato. The buns were then broiled until the cheese melted and the hot dogs heated. This wasn't a typical choice for patients and didn't meet the requirements of a balanced meal.

After his team discussed it, they reluctantly gave their consent. After all, he had a wife at home who would cook for him. They realized that Ken had never cooked a full meal before, so even this simple recipe would challenge his cooking ability.

Armed with his list, Ken wheeled to the local grocery store, purchased whole wheat buns, a package of processed cheese, hot dogs, and a tomato. Getting into the spirit of the adventure, he spontaneously added a can of tomato sauce and a green pepper to his basket.

Hey, why not make them extra special? he asked himself.

With a bulging plastic grocery bag hanging from the handle on the back of his wheelchair, he returned ready to begin. He carefully prepared the Cheese Dreams, serving each bun out, enjoying every mouthful, and savouring the first meal he had ever prepared and cooked from scratch that hadn't been heated from a can or frozen in a box.

For years, Ken talked about how delicious those Cheese Dreams were and occasionally gave me pointers when I prepared them.

The doctor had suspended Ken's driver's license, and an evaluation was required to have it unsuspended. Since driving was an integral part of Ken's identity, I was concerned that a failure could negatively affect his morale. I asked everyone to pray, knowing that he wouldn't always be content sitting in the passenger seat.

The tests were independently conducted at another rehab facility where the doctors checked his reflexes and the strength of his right leg. After waiting a tense two weeks for the results to arrive in the mail, Ken quickly tore open the envelope and heaved a sigh of relief to read that he'd passed. Praise the Lord!

He was even more pleased to learn that he'd done so well that his driver's license was reinstated without any further stipulations—no hand controls or extra equipment were required. However, for safety, Ken ordered and installed hand controls in his truck.

A week or two later when I answered the phone, Ken's excited voice greeted me. His discharge date was finalized for Friday, February 25, and he would continue his therapy as an outpatient at Credit Valley Hospital, a short drive from our house.

This news definitely called for a celebration, and a surprise welcome home party seemed appropriate. On Ken's final day, so I could remain at home to greet our guests, Ken Mercer brought him, his luggage, and his skis home from Lyndhurst.

Loved ones filled the house, a "Welcome Home" banner hung in the living room, the chandelier held a bouquet of balloons, and a hot buffet meal was spread over the dining room table while we patiently waited for Ken to arrive. Cheers greeted him as he came through the door, and by the look on his face I knew he was surprised. Gathered together were our family and friends: the ones who had prayed diligently for us, people whose faith had never wavered, folks who had supported us in every way imaginable. As our loved ones had gathered together on the darkest day of our lives, it was fitting that this victorious moment be shared with everyone.

Chapter Sixteen

THE CHALLENGE OF CHANGES

Ken treated his disability as a challenge to be conquered daily. To Ken's mind, his life had become the equivalent of living on a black diamond ski trail, every move a challenge. Getting out of bed, dressing, cutting food, getting into the car were all a struggle, but he also enjoyed the satisfaction of overcoming each obstacle, viewing each achievement as a well-deserved victory.

He used his walker or a cane in the house, but because the ground was uneven he used his wheelchair outdoors. To get into his truck, he wheeled to where it was parked, opened the tailgate, stood up, and sat on it, then folded his wheelchair, and with the help of his lap slid it into the truck bed. He then stood back up, closed the tailgate, and walked to the driver's door by holding onto the side of the truck.

Before Ken climbed back behind the steering wheel for the first time, Rob felt that Ken should have a practice run. On a bright sunny day, Ken drove slowly down the driveway, with Rob sitting shotgun beside him, making sure he drove safely.

The next day, after a successful ride with Rob, Ken decided to try a solo trip to the local pool and asked me to pack a swimsuit and towel. I watched from the window and waved goodbye as Ken drove solo for the first time, bringing tears to my eyes. Seeing the joy reflected on Ken's face as he realized his worst fears weren't becoming reality, I couldn't help but also smile and whisper a prayer of thanksgiving.

Ken was back in the driver's seat—wild horses couldn't have held him back.

Ken Rides Again

I had made it! I was back in the saddle! Sliding into the seat was like being welcomed by an old friend. Boy, it sure felt good to be out in my old gold truck. Thank You, Lord! What a great time of year for new things—spring. I was so glad to be outside again, feeling the sun on my shoulders.

Things were a little different from the last time I had ridden my beauty. A wheelchair lay in the back, a blue accessible parking permit sat on the dashboard, and a cell phone rested in my pocket. Well, a lot more than that had changed. It was funny; in my dreams I could walk, run, even play hockey, and it felt so real—so good. It was always a shock to wake up and realize that I'd been dreaming.

Sometimes I wished the reality I was living with was the dream—that it hadn't really happened. What used to take moments to do, things I hardly gave a thought about, took such an effort now. Walking up a few stairs felt like I had a refrigerator strapped to my back. My wheelchair only weighed about twenty pounds, but it felt heavier, triple that weight—even more. Every muscle was strained to its limit. I'd never worked that hard in my life, and I knew what hard work was! I kept waiting for things to get easier, but then when they did I pushed myself harder, always straining to do more.

There's an old saying: "Don't worry about biting off more than you can chew; your mouth is probably a whole lot bigger than you think." That was my philosophy. You don't know what you're capable of until you try. Someday I would get there, but I wasn't ready to settle for less than my best. Reaching my full potential was important to me, so I wouldn't have to be too dependent on others.

I was thankful to escape the confines of the house, and I knew Sharon was thankful, too. She tried not to show it, but I knew she appreciated having the house to herself once in a while. When she watched my progress from the window, making sure I'd made it into the truck okay, and then blew me a kiss as she waved goodbye, I felt loved. I was glad to have her by my side and didn't know what I would do without her.

She reminded me to grab my cell phone on the way out. I had purchased one the day before, as we thought it wise. I'd also had to ask

Sharon to pack a gym bag with a swimsuit and an old towel and carry it out to the truck for me, so I wasn't totally independent—yet.

Actually, something else had changed: I would have to stop riding the truck on empty. This always drove Sharon nuts, which spurred me to push the gas gauge needle to the limit. She got uptight and started nagging me to fill up when there was still plenty left, usually at least an eighth of a tank. She was beautiful when she was angry. Her eyes snapped and flashed, her cheeks grew pink, and she started talking faster. Then she'd cross her arms and give me the silent treatment, hunching her shoulders and turning to gaze out the passenger window. She thought the world would end when the gas did. I never actually ran out.

Well, hardly ever. There had been a close call a few years back when we'd been heading north on Highway 10.

"There's a gas station just up ahead on the right," she had said in a calm, innocent voice.

She'd noticed the gauge was hovering at empty. I had noticed it, too, and had already planned on stopping at the same station. But then I changed my mind and chose to have some fun instead.

I decided to fiddle with the radio and slightly slow down just when I'd have to pull into the station. It had worked perfectly and I saw Sharon stiffen when I accelerated and sailed by. After that, she was really eyeing the gauge and struggling to keep silent. Seeing her cross her arms had made me want to burst into laughter.

The next station had only been a couple of miles ahead, but I'd found it difficult to keep nonchalant as I had been sure we'd run out any second. Boy, if that had happened I would've never heard the end of it!

I attempted to start up a conversation with her, but it failed because my mind was preoccupied. My family had two rules: no punching in the head, ever, and if anyone runs out of gas the driver has to walk for more, no passing off the dirty deed.

Relief washed over me when I saw the next station on the horizon, and this time I wasn't driving by. I eased off the gas, preparing to turn in, and my heart dropped into my stomach when the truck stalled. The driveway ran slightly downhill and I had just enough momentum to coast in beside the pump.

Only one problem presented itself: I had steered to the wrong side. The pump was on the passenger side and the gas cap was on my side.

Sharon hadn't said a word. She just sat staring straight ahead out the windshield as I put the truck in neutral, turned the wheel slightly, got out, and pushed it back. Then I pushed it forward to the correct side.

She didn't bother to get out of the truck, of course. She knew the rule: the driver walks.

The station had been run by an attendant and when the guy strolled out, he asked me why I had pushed the truck over instead of driving it. He obviously hadn't noticed that the truck wasn't running when I coasted in. I gave him a look that said, *Don't you know anything?*

"Because I'm out of gas," I said instead.

Sharon and I had a good, hearty laugh over it later—after she had cooled down. The joke turned out to be on myself.

It looked like I wouldn't ever pull that prank again now, because this driver can't walk—but I can still drive!

It was nice of Rob to have come with me on my first trial run the day before. At first he had seemed nervous, but he relaxed when I stopped the truck quickly at a red light.

I didn't know what I would have done without Rob's support over the past six months. He was one of the few people who treated me the same after my injury as before. I didn't understand why some people thought I was less of a person just because I was sitting in a wheelchair.

Rob visited me as often as he could, and I was always happy to see him. Along with a humorous story or anecdote to share, he brought a relaxed and cheerful atmosphere. Oh, I knew Rob was worried about me; I could sense his uneasiness, as brothers can't hide everything from each other, even if they try. But I always knew he had my back and was looking out for me in ways I couldn't. For example, he had been thinking about employment options for me long before I could bring myself to face the issue. I was so thankful that I'd been blessed with a brother like Rob, glad I'd been blessed with my whole family. They were all there for me and didn't let me down when I was at my lowest.

When I got home from my swim that afternoon, Sharon and I were going to register James for kindergarten at the same Christian school I had attended. Unbelievably, I thought a couple of my former teachers were still teaching there. Sharon had been saving our monthly "baby bonus" government payments since James was born, so the first year's tuition was already saved. Christian education was important to us both and we knew the Lord was leading us to take a step of faith to send the boys. We had faith that the Lord would help us afford the next year's tuition just as He had helped us financially over the past few months.

The sun was shining and the roads dry on the way to the pool, so I didn't think getting from the truck into the recreation centre would be a problem. After I'd done this on my own once or twice I'd bring James along with me. He loved splashing in the pool and was nice, cheerful company. I loved swimming, too, but for different reasons. The warm water relieved my aches and pains and the exercise was beneficial to helping me sleep soundly.

I was sure I'd discover a few positive effects of my injury over time, but I was already aware of one: I was thankful for the extra time I could spend with James and John. They were so young that in the future I thought they might not remember how I'd been before my injury, when I had been able to toss them in the air and swing them around. I hoped they remembered how much time we were able to spend together now.

Sharon Sorts Out the Details

Ken had a busy schedule: swimming each morning at our local pool, physiotherapy several times a week at Credit Valley Hospital, regular check-ups at Lyndhurst, and weekly massage appointments. Soon he would start an AutoCAD course at Sheridan College for two evenings a week. This course challenged Ken on several levels: learning drafting techniques from scratch, mastering the program itself, and learning the basics of how to use a computer, all while taking notes left-handed. It would be another eight months before his hand strengthened enough so he could write with his dominant right hand.

Along with these activities, the time had come for Ken to pick up the reins of his business once again. Alex and Ken Mercer had been life-savers by stepping in to complete the several unfinished projects Ken had started before his injury. Now Ken had to start overseeing his projects from home rather than from the jobsite.

After a few months, this proved to be ineffective and strengthened his resolve to continue studying to become an architectural designer. Over the next couple of years, Ken gradually used his construction contacts to gain design clients and he slowly turned over the construction side of the company to Peter and Alex.

When Ken had an errand to run, even for business, James quite often tagged along. He was Ken's little helper and assisted him by opening doors and carrying his briefcase. Where Ken used to include the boys in tasks around the house or in his yard work, he now brought them along to his appointments. Maintaining a professional image before his clients didn't take priority over demonstrating to his boys that they were an important part of his life. Over the years, James and John spent countless hours waiting with Ken for their turn in building departments across the city, becoming favourites with the clerks.

Around this time, Ken and I re-evaluated when he used his wheelchair, walker, and cane. In the house he used his walker or cane, but this proved inconvenient because he couldn't carry anything in his hands. He used a cane to walk into church, but this meant, due to a lack of endurance, that he couldn't stand and visit with his friends afterward. Tripping and falling were a constant hazard, because he still wasn't steady on his feet. After consulting with Ken's doctor, we all agreed it would be best for Ken to use his wheelchair full-time. This actually increased his freedom, as he could carry items on his lap and get to destinations more quickly and easily, which conserved his energy for other things. It also eased his worry of falling.

After a few months, we had a system worked out. When Ken arrived home, he left his wheelchair in the back of the truck and used an old wheelchair which had large treads on the tires to wheel to the back door. Then he stood, opened the door, climbed four stairs to our kitchen, and sat down in his indoor wheelchair. This way, Ken could bypass the ramp, which was too steep for him to use by himself anyway. It also saved me the hassle of carrying wheelchairs in and out of the house.

It took me a month or two to realize that my doubts at Christmastime had been groundless. Ken had plenty of activities to keep him busy and I found it a blessing to have him home.

However, there was one issue I hadn't counted on having to get used to: learning to sleep in the same bed again. As Ken's legs grew more muscular, he occasionally had muscle spasms in the night. While fast asleep on his side, breathing in an even rhythm, his knees would forcefully jerk up to his chest without warning. It wouldn't have been a problem if he slept by himself, but I was usually in the way. Being sound asleep myself, I was unaware of the impending danger. My legs were bruised black and blue from being hit by his knees almost every night.

It took a few weeks before I realized he gave a sharp exhalation of breath a split second before the jack-knife trick. Even in my sleep, if Ken exhaled sharply I'd instantly react by rolling out of the way in one quick motion. Ken, unaware of his hazardous behaviour, slept right through it, usually just changing position.

One night before we fell asleep, he took a quick, deep breath to sneeze. He was puzzled when I instinctively flung myself to safety on the other side of the bed. He wondered what was wrong with me, and when I explained he didn't seem to believe me. He excused his behaviour by saying that his legs jerked slightly when he dreamed about playing hockey and then gave me that "you'll get over it" look. I was surprised he didn't wake up each morning exhausted from his nocturnal hockey games.

Each spring I attended a weekend ladies retreat with my girlfriends, but this year I wasn't sure if I should go. Ken reassured me that he could manage the boys by himself for one weekend and encouraged me to sign up.

Looking back, I don't remember very much about the weekend. My journal reports that the keynote speaker had an inspiring testimony and that the Holy Spirit was present in a powerful way, but most of the details have faded from my memory.

Except one. The moment I remember as clearly as if it happened yesterday was the very last session when communion was served. I've taken communion hundreds of times before, but this day something special happened, something I'll never forget.

While praying silently, thanking the Lord for dying on the cross and forgiving my sins, I followed the leader's direction to eat the bread, remembering how Christ had sacrificed His body for us. I had the wafer halfway to my open mouth when God spoke to my heart. God had never spoken to me this clearly before; it was like He bent down and whispered directly into my ear.

"I will heal Ken's body," He said in an almost audible voice.

I was taken completely off-guard and couldn't swallow the wafer because of the sobs I tried unsuccessfully to stifle; they kept escaping, disturbing the quiet atmosphere around me. God's presence surrounded me—it was so real. When I heard God's voice, Ken hadn't been on my mind. I had been focused on thanking Him for saving me.

My faith soared to new heights and I became convinced that God would completely heal Ken very soon. God's voice was so powerful, and I was so sure the time was near, that I was impatient to return home to see if anything had already changed in Ken physically.

After I returned home and didn't detect any change in Ken, I was disappointed, but I decided to be patient and wait. I never told anyone what had happened to me. However, I kept it in my heart as something special to watch for.

As the years went by and Ken's progress gradually slowed and plateaued, I remembered this moment and wondered if God hadn't spoken to me after all. I wondered if I had imagined hearing His voice, if it had been just a natural result of what I had been longing for. Whenever I'd have these doubts and review again what I had experienced, I'd return to the same conclusion: it had not been my imagination. God had spoken clearly to me, and someday, whether in this life or the next, God would completely heal Ken's body.

Chapter Seventeen

FREEDOM REDEFINED

Ken's determination, which had made him stand out as an athlete, came to his assistance in the arena of physiotherapy. Where others got tired or lost hope, Ken kept going, never complaining or giving up but plodding on, always striving to do better. I could also tell Ken was working hard because he started to look more muscular, not like a typical quadriplegic. The muscles on his arms became more defined, his legs more stable and reliable, and his gait steadier.

Ken loved spending time outside and always brought the boys out with him. John, who had just turned three, was very obedient, doing exactly what Ken asked—except one day he put Ken in an awkward position. We had a large maple tree in our front yard with a sturdy branch at the perfect height for Ken to work on his chin-ups. He'd wheel his chair into the shade of the tree beside the trunk, stand, and take a few steps while holding the overhead branch to his favourite spot where it was easiest to grasp. Standing and stretching his back to work out the kinks felt good. Then he'd flex his arm muscles and try one or two chin-ups.

Ken had done this numerous times without incident while the boys ran around him playing on the lawn.

One day, John ran up to Ken and threw his arms around his legs to hug him, but Ken had been wearing track pants and John's hug caused Ken's pants to fall to his ankles.

Wondering what to do, Ken held fast to the branch over his head, on his front lawn, in his underwear. His pants prevented him from taking a step, and if he released his hold on the branch to bend over, he would fall. Ken's only hope was to convince John of the importance of pulling up his dad's pants. John struggled to work them up his hairy shins, and with some squirming on Ken's part he managed to get them within reach. That was the end of the chin-ups for that day. Next time, Ken made sure his pants' drawstring was tightly tied.

As the weather became warmer, our thoughts turned to heading north once again, and the long Victoria Day weekend in May was to be our first trip back. I packed our station wagon to the roof, locked up the house, and strapped the kids into the back seat. Ken got in the driver's seat, we donned our sunglasses, and then we rushed to join the stampeding herd of traffic heading in the same direction.

Partway up, forgotten memories about the last time I'd been there came flooding back. I was unprepared for this surge of emotions. In the busyness of getting ready, I hadn't prepared myself for returning.

Suddenly, another hurdle loomed before me. The cottage overflowed with memories of my carefree, galloping, pre-injured Ken. Would the changes ever end? I became unusually quiet and Ken sensed my struggle, wondering if I was okay. He had recognized much earlier than I that this weekend could be difficult.

After the first few hours, the worst was over and I could join in the fun with everyone else. The weather was warm, like a July weekend, but the water was still icy cold. This didn't stop Alex and me from pulling out the water skis and taking turns skiing around the lake with Ken sitting in the boat spotting for us.

Afterward, when Alex and I were flopped on the dock exhausted, Ken announced that he wanted to put on the skis and give them a whirl. Alex was in agreement with me that this was far beyond Ken's capabilities. How could Ken think he could water ski when he could barely walk? Never mind coping with the cold water.

His stubbornness was certainly evident, but I refused to give in. Not like years earlier, when Ken had insisted that I teach him to slalom ski immediately after learning to water ski. The only way to stop Ken from pestering us was to put the skis away out of his sight.

Ken and Alex talked about the changes needed to make the cottage accessible. With a slight modification to the cottage porch, and by extending the dock farther around the shore, Ken could ride his ATV from the porch onto the dock by the water. Ken offered to pay for the lumber if Alex built the extensions, and in a few weeks one more hurdle was overcome.

Rob to the Rescue

I was busy working in my office in Georgetown, talking on the phone, when the second line rang. After putting my first call on hold, I answered it and heard Ken's voice say, "Hi, Rob. Are you busy?"

"Yes, I'm busy," I said. "I'm on the other line. What's the matter?"

"Never mind. I'll call you back later." He hung up, but hardly two minutes had gone by before Ken called back again. "Are you still busy?"

"What do you mean, *am I still busy?* I'm on the phone. What do you want? What's the matter?"

"You know the gas station down the road where they sell cars? Can you drive there and then walk up the hill a little ways into the bush?"

"Why is that?" I asked.

"Oh, because… my ATV is stuck."

I then realized that Ken was calling from his cell phone.

After quickly ending my first call, I closed my office, drove to the gas station, and started walking up the tree-covered hill as Ken had directed. Luckily I had on my old shoes with the good treads, but still my legs started to burn, as the hill was steep.

Stopping to catch my breath, I heard a voice say, "Hiya, Rob."

There was Ken, with a big grin on his face just ahead of me. He sat on his ATV, which was unfortunately wedged between two trees. He'd been driving down the hill through the forest and lost traction, causing him to slide down a few feet and get stuck. Judging by the ruts under his back wheels, he'd tried his best to free himself but just couldn't manage it.

With a lot of manoeuvring, groaning, and wrestling against gravity, we managed to move the ATV back onto the trail. Ken then continued on his way down the path, turning in his seat to wave.

"Thanks, Rob," he called over his shoulder. "I owe you one… and don't tell Sharon!"

Returning to the truck, I recalled a strange conversation Ken and I had had about a year ago, before his injury. We had been with our hockey buddies and it was late at night after playing a game. We'd all been pumped up, adrenaline still surging, and decided to head to a doughnut shop before going home. I can't remember how the conversation started, perhaps someone came in using a wheelchair, but we started to discuss what it would be like to be a paraplegic or quadriplegic. We had wondered if life would still be worth living and if we'd still want to be alive. We sat around the table and pondered this deep psychological question.

I can't remember exactly what Ken thought, but we all agreed the whole concept was scary, like living in a nightmare, and not pleasant to talk about. Now here was Ken, living out our conversation—living out what we'd all feared.

Strangely, Ken's injury didn't just happen to him; it happened to our whole family. All of our lives were impacted more than I could ever have imagined. Nothing really bad had ever happened to me before, and I was stunned at the degree to which it affected me. Carey said I wouldn't always—couldn't always—be there to assist Ken and should learn to leave him in God's hands, but Ken was always in my peripheral vision. I was always wondering and worrying about how decisions I made would affect him. Carey and I talked about relocating, but I couldn't help feeling that I'd be letting Ken down. I was working on this but still had a long way to go.

Ken was an inspiration to me. Here he was, exploring and enjoying the outdoors. Sure, he had gotten stuck and I'd had to drop everything to rescue him, but he wasn't sitting at home in the dark feeling sorry for himself. He was busy at school learning a new trade and talking about starting up an architectural design company. He hadn't quit on God when times got tough. He just kept on going.

Over the last while, I've learned that God is always faithful. After Ken's accident, I thought his future looked hopeless, that nothing would go well for him again. But I was wrong. God had opened doors to opportunities Ken would never have had before, and he bravely walked through each one. Already he was talking to other people with disabilities and sharing what God had done for him. He was showing others

God's love and giving himself to others. He wasn't content to always be on the receiving end.

I noticed that others didn't treat Ken like a disabled person. Maybe this was because he didn't act like one. When he talked to someone, he leaned back in his wheelchair, kicked his feet out in front, and put his hands behind his head, transforming his wheelchair into an easy chair. This put others at ease and also destroyed their misconceptions about wheelchairs.

He was talking about trying out wheelchair basketball once his arms were stronger, and he showed me a magazine article about a scuba diving program for people with disabilities. He was enjoying the wonderful gift of life God had given him, even if there were challenges along the way.

When I opened the truck door that day by the gas station, the thought came to me that I was proud of Ken. I was proud of the way he had learned to focus on his capabilities instead of his limitations. I was proud of the way he had leaned on God when others would have rejected their faith and felt God had let them down. I was proud of the way he was reaching out to others rather than always expecting to be served.

Most of all, I was proud to be his brother. Sure, I questioned his sanity in roaming around the bush by himself, but you had to give the guy credit: he had accepted the cards God dealt him and was playing the best game he could with what he had.

Chapter Eighteen

OUR NEW LIFE

Acts 3:8 says, *"He jumped to his feet and began to walk. Then he went with them into the temple courts, walking and jumping, and praising God."* The King James Version describes this man leaping, and you can picture it, can't you? A man, crippled from birth, longing to join in but always neglected, left sitting on the sidelines, sighing when he is once again overlooked and forgotten. But suddenly his wildest dream comes true. He has replayed this dream in his mind again and again but never dared to hope for it. He's healed! He jumps to his feet and walks, leaps, and praises God.

His excitement rubs off on me and I want to join him in his happy dance.

In my idle moments, this is what I dreamed and fantasized about over and over. This is what I prayed for and waited for—to see Ken jumping and leaping and praising God. I dreamed of running into his arms, of him lifting me up and swinging me around, of each of us laughing and crying at the same time. Walking hand in hand, I would look up into his laughing eyes and we'd be young and carefree again.

God was certainly powerful enough to heal Ken, and it is scriptural to faithfully and expectantly wait for our prayers to be answered. So why doesn't it happen? How long will it take? Was I mistaken when I heard God tell me so clearly that Ken would be healed? What was I supposed to do now? Should I hang my dreams back up in the closet and close the door? Should I shrug my shoulders, turn my back, and walk away? Or should I continue to wait and pray for more patience?

I longed for a glimmer of hope, to see a flicker of light in the darkness, to be reassured that the end was drawing near and my life wouldn't always be this way. Sometimes I even found it hard to read about Jesus' miracles in the Bible, because everyone He touched was healed. Even in his hometown of Nazareth, where unbelief ran rampant, He healed a few sick people.

I know He still heals today, but why not us? Why not Ken?

The recovery God granted Ken was miraculous. We couldn't deny it! But I found it difficult to deal with and accept his limitations. Ken was able to look after his own personal care, but the weight of responsibility of caring for our small family lay heavily on my shoulders. I kept wishing that the calendar would flip ahead to an easier time, a time when adjusting to our new life would be over, to a time when life would be easier.

It took me years to fully accept the road I was destined to walk.

As time slowly marched along, my strong desire and longing for Ken's healing gradually diminished. It took a back seat in my life and became a lower priority on my prayer list, but it never completely went away.

In struggling with the issue of Ken not being totally, one hundred percent healed, I also struggled with our relationship. I had to unwrap and get to know this new and different version of Ken I found myself married to. Instead of looking up into his eyes, tilting my head back to accommodate his six-foot height, I now looked down at the top of his head. His strong, roughly calloused hands had transformed into softer, tenderer versions. I missed being enfolded in a masculine bear hug. Areas where he had been confident and sure of himself now revealed a fragility I had never witnessed before. He looked at me with questioning eyes, unsure of himself and seeking reassurance from me. The tables were turned, as Ken had usually been the one to reassure me. Now I had to step up and be the strong one supporting him. But who would reassure and comfort me?

Prior to Ken's injury, our fun times were spent outside, walking, skiing, biking, and being active together. Without these pastimes in my life, I was left with an empty void. I realized that one of the reasons I had been drawn to Ken was the physically active times we shared. We were left with a gaping hole in our relationship. How could we fill it?

We were on a new level, one we had never experienced before. The man I had fallen in love with had changed overnight into someone I'd never met before. I found myself wondering, *Where do we go from here? How do we find our way?*

Ken and I were frustrated because when we shared these challenges with a pastor or counsellor and asked for help or prayer, they simply counselled us to focus on the recovery Ken had been blessed with and would pray for Ken's complete physical healing. The issues we were dealing with were beyond their comprehension and expertise.

Others thought we should be thankful that we still had one another and move on, thankful that Ken wasn't totally paralyzed. In their eyes, Ken's needs took a higher priority than my own.

We felt very alone in learning how to deal with Ken's disability in regards to how it affected our marriage.

A few years after Ken's injury, when the boys were old enough to be left on their own for an hour or two, Ken and I decided to do some Christmas shopping at our local mall. Unfortunately, just before parking in the handicapped section, it started to rain—heavily. We sat in Ken's truck and watched the rain bouncing off the pavement. It came down by the bucketful, with no sign of letting up, and we didn't have an umbrella.

"There's no sense in us both getting wet," Ken said. "I'll get out my wheelchair and you make a run for the door."

This sounded like a sensible plan, so I put up the hood on my jacket and dashed to the entrance, waiting for Ken outside under the overhang. He had managed to get into his wheelchair in record time and wasn't too far behind me, but he was definitely wetter than I was.

A gentleman was standing nearby who opened the door for Ken. "Merry Christmas," he said.

I was walking close behind Ken and looked up at the gentleman, ready to return his holiday greeting. But instead of a jolly expression, I was greeted with a glare. His upper lip turned up at one side and he raised his chin, looking down his nose at me, like I was a worm who had just crawled up onto the wet pavement. His eyes bored into mine, transmitting a message of disgust.

I felt like I'd just been punched in the stomach and had to blink to keep the tears at bay. Christmas music still played over the store's sound system, the Christmas tree nearby still had the lights lit, but for me the holiday spirit had dissipated. My outing was ruined. What had I done to deserve such hostility?

I then realized he had probably watched us come in from the rain and had witnessed my run to keep dry while my husband struggled with his wheelchair.

At this point in our relationship, I was struggling with our altered roles. Ken had always been my strong protector, making me feel cherished and loved. Since his injury I had become the protector and provider, ensuring that he was cared for. We were working hard to reverse our roles back to husband and wife, rather than disabled person and caregiver. This gentleman stranger, in one long look, denied me the right to feel loved and cherished by my husband and judged me as being selfish and inconsiderate. Unfortunately, he echoed the attitude of many people who viewed me as someone whose sole purpose was to serve and assist Ken.

Do you feel alone? Are you longing to feel loved and cherished? Let me tell you loud and clear that you are. God loves and cherishes you like no one else can. You deserve to feel God's love, to feel Him cherishing you. Like Ken wanted me to feel protected, God wants to be your strong tower—the safe place you can run into. The Lord will be your champion when you feel alone and neglected, if you let Him. The reason you can trust Him is because He loves you so much. He sent His only son, Jesus Christ, who was crucified as an atonement for your sin, because He loves you. No one else can ever love you this completely, this perfectly.

Have you ever noticed how a grandparent loves their grandchild? My parents treat my children quite differently than they did me. They are indulgent with James and John, wanting to make life easy, jumping in to remove every obstacle. Parents know their children's potential, and it's their parental task to refine and enhance their character, enabling them to fully develop into the best people they can be. Grandparents get to lavishly pour out all their love without being hindered by this responsibility.

Sometimes I wish God loved me like a grandparent, removed all trials from my path, answered all my prayer requests, and made the way as easy as possible, but thankfully He doesn't love me this way. He loves me like a *father*.

He has a plan for you, a multicoloured, bigger-than-life image in His mind of what He wants you to become. To achieve this goal, He steers your life not towards the smooth downhill road with no bumps or curves, but toward the more difficult road which will unfold to reveal the handpicked lessons chosen specifically for you. Even though it's not the easiest pathway, in the end it will prove to be the better one.

I've also learned that God is more interested in developing us and helping us mature spiritually than in healing our physical bodies. He uses challenges and trials to refine us and prepare us for the greater plan He has ordained for us. If we look at ourselves from God's perspective, our physical bodies are only temporal; after we're done with them, they'll be left behind when we ascend to heaven, but our spiritual selves will last for eternity.

Developing our spiritual side, sometimes at the expense of our physical comfort, may be God's plan for us. God doesn't orchestrate bad things to happen to us, but He *allows* them so that we'll grow closer to Him, to strengthen our faith, and as a means to learn more about Him.

I remember when James was very young and I had just turned on my curling iron, which sat on my dressing table, slowly heating. James reached out his hand to touch it and I said, "No, James. It's hot." He looked at me, then turned his head back, looking again at the curling iron. Knowing he wouldn't listen to my warning, but go ahead and grab the shiny hot barrel, I made a split-second decision to allow him to touch it and not reach over him to move it out of his reach. It wasn't yet hot enough to seriously burn him, but hot enough to make him jump—and he did! He looked back at me, rubbing his sore hand, hurt that I hadn't intervened. However, it also hurt me to teach the hard lesson.

Later, when he was near the stove and I told him to be careful because it was hot, he immediately backed away. At the cottage, when the woodstove was fired up and scorching, he heeded my warning. I allowed the small discomfort of a hot curling iron because I loved him and wanted him to learn to obey me.

God treats us the same way. He allows the difficult and hard times in our lives because He loves us. He has a greater plan than we can comprehend. He wants us to learn and grow, not stagnate by easy living. It says in Psalm 119:71, *"It was good for me to be afflicted so that I might learn your decrees."* God wants us to learn to discern and hear His voice—to heed His warnings.

In looking back over the years, I can see the Lord's hand guiding Ken and me, preparing us for 1993. His hand was evident in the timing of when we purchased our house, in motivating us to quickly pay down our mortgage, in deciding when the children came along, even in the timing of our upstairs addition which was completed only a few weeks prior to Ken's injury. God's hand directed Ken to wear his hardhat that day, which probably saved his life and most certainly protected him from a brain injury. I can see God's hand in the fact that I was away at the cottage. An employee who was working at our house that August day answered our home phone and was horrified to hear a hysterical voice wrongly reporting that Ken had died.

It wasn't until a year or two after Ken's injury that he told me about his prayer the night before he fell. He'd had the house to himself, had finished working on a motor he was trying to fix, when he had lain prostrate on the living room carpet. He had been consumed with the need to pray for his two sons.

"Lord," he'd prayed, "do whatever You desire in me to ensure my boys come to know You."

His heart's cry was for James and John to experience salvation as he had. We don't know if Ken's fall was part of answering this prayer or not, but we do know that God has answered that prayer. Today both our boys serve God wholeheartedly.

Adapting to our new life wasn't easy and we had to find new ways to spend time together. In the years to come we learned to scuba dive, bought kayaks, went on road trips instead of ski trips, found accessible walking trails, and purchased another ATV for me. I even learned the intricacies of pull-starting a snowmobile so we could ride together. Yes, Ken had to forego some sports he had once enjoyed, but instead he tried new sports: sailing, sit-skiing, scuba diving, dogsledding, even parasailing. Wheelchair basketball and wheelchair tennis also kept Ken physically active.

I hesitate to suggest reasons why the Lord allowed that August day to change our lives so drastically, but Ken and I are both changed. We have matured spiritually and learned lessons we'd never have learned without hardship. We can now empathize with others who struggle with the same issues we experienced.

After Ken's injury, due to necessity, we stepped off the spinning carousel of busyness and refocused our priorities. Emotionally and physically I was burnt out, barely capable of coping with everyday life; I had nothing left over to nurture insignificant fluff. We had to ditch time-wasters that weren't imperative to our family's well-being, as we opted to focus our energy on keeping our home happy.

We noticed the difference when we compared our lives with others. Our contemporaries replaced reading bedtime stories together with letting the kids watch a bedtime video alone. They were too busy chauffeuring kids to various sporting events to enjoy evening mealtimes together. They replaced attending church services with dance lessons.

Our children have grown into strong young men and having a physically challenged father has enabled them to be caring towards others and gentle in their mannerisms. A friend mentioned to me that Ken never took the boys skiing, never went biking with them, and never ran beside them in a park. But instead of missing out, they were *more* blessed by the values Ken taught them. Ken demonstrated how to accept hard times without becoming bitter, how to laugh even though it hurts, and how to not get angry with God when things don't go your way.

Life, even one with a disability, has so much to offer. Ken didn't miss out on the most important facets of life—love, a supportive family, friendships, and a relationship with Jesus. These years of trial strengthened our faith in the Lord. From an early age, we both trusted in Jesus and had faith in Him. But after learning the lessons God had planned for us, our faith grew stronger, to a level we couldn't have achieved without these trials.

If I had been given the choice of walking down this path or not, would I have chosen to walk it? Probably not—okay, certainly not. But I'm thankful the Lord took the decision out of my hands and made it for me. 1 Peter 1:6–7 says,

> *In all this you greatly rejoice, though now for a little while you may have had to suffer grief in all kinds of trials. These have come so that the proven genuineness of your faith—of greater worth than gold, which perishes even though refined by fire—may result in praise, glory and honor when Jesus Christ is revealed.*

The Lord doesn't enjoy mapping out the hard road He's chosen for us, but He allows it for our own good in order to refine us. As it says in Lamentations 3:33, *"For he does not willingly bring affliction or grief to anyone."*

Isaiah 30:18 says, *"Yet the Lord longs to be gracious to you; therefore he will rise up to show you compassion. For the Lord is a God of justice. Blessed are all who wait for him!"* Did you catch that? Because He loves us so much, He *longs* to show us compassion. He is waiting for exactly the right moment.

I have a mental picture of God sitting on His throne, not leaning back—majestically passive, slightly bored—as He watches events unfold before Him; I see Him perched on the edge of His seat, leaning forward with His hand outstretched, longing to remove obstacles from our path. It is for our own good that He holds back, waiting for just the right moment.

Do you have a trial or crisis towering over you, threatening to crush and drown you? Lying awake in the dark, do unanswerable questions swirl around you like a swarm of bees? Does stress make drawing your next breath difficult? Are you looking for someone to put your trust in, someone to wipe away your tears? Look no further. Jesus is waiting for you to reach out and take hold of His extended hand. All you need to do is lean back into His arms and simply trust Him. Psalm 40:1–2 says,

I waited patiently for the Lord; he turned to me and heard my cry. He lifted me out of the slimy pit, out of the mud and mire; he set my feet on a rock and gave me a firm place to stand.

The Lord heard the psalmist's cry for help, He heard my cry, and He will hear yours. He longs for you to trust Him.

Chapter Nineteen

TRUE HEALING AT LAST

Eighteen months have elapsed since I penned the first eighteen chapters of this book. When I thought our story was ready to be told, I didn't realize a page would turn and another chapter would need to be written.

On September 22, 2015, twenty-two years after Ken's spinal cord injury and after our boys were grown, I received another phone call that dramatically impacted my life.

Ken had been planning this trip for over a year. He would fly to the Netherlands, visit with his extended family for one week, then meet up with several friends in France for a tour of World War II memorials.

He never made it to France.

While staying with his cousin in Maastricht, just five days after his arrival, he suffered a severe stroke. After dinner, mid-conversation, he slumped over in his wheelchair. He was rushed by ambulance to a nearby state-of-the-art hospital where doctors and nurses gave him the best care available. Ken's cousin called overseas with the news that the stroke had been a heavy one. Ken could not move or speak, but he was conscious.

I have a new reference point in my life now—prior to Ken's stroke and after Ken's stroke. In the twenty years prior to Ken's stroke, I would love to report that everything slowly became easier and easier, that as time marched along we coped well and adapted just fine. But I can't say that. I trusted God in my life, knew that He would meet our needs and would be there to help and protect us, but something was missing.

Claiming victory after Ken's spinal cord injury eluded me. I hung on but was frustrated most of the time and easily stressed out. Working

Sharon Faber

full-time and taking care of my household emotionally exhausted me. I toughed it out, mostly in my own strength. Really, I was just keeping the status quo, waiting for things to get better. I wasn't satisfied with how my life had turned out and I couldn't find contentment.

God had given me peace, but I needed something more. The question was, what?

Twenty-six-year-old James and I booked a last-minute flight to the Netherlands while John stayed home to look after things while we were away.

The stroke had occurred on the left side of Ken's brain, in the area that affects language and movement on the right side. He lost all movement below the level of his spinal cord injury, returning to the degree of paralysis he'd initially suffered after his fall from the ladder. His stroke was so severe that he couldn't talk at all; even indicating a yes or no was impossible. When asked a question, Ken would just lower his eyebrows and look confused. He could hear and understand but was unable to communicate what he felt and thought.

I was older and more mature, but I was surprised to be facing all the same fears I'd experienced so long ago. Memories of "the first time" came flooding back and I asked the same questions. Would Ken survive? How could we cope with this? Would Ken become my shackle? I was afraid, once again, that the level of care Ken required would consume me and take away my freedom.

This time, a new fear gripped me—depression. In learning to cope with his injury, Ken had waded through the dark waters of depression twenty years earlier. I was afraid I couldn't cope with another bout.

Suffering a major heart attack about nine years earlier had left Ken's heart in bad shape. His cardiologist had forewarned that another heart event would prove fatal. We had tried to prepare ourselves for the possibility of Ken's sudden death, but dealing with further debilitation hadn't occurred to us.

Ten days later, as soon as Ken as able to sit upright for a few hours at a time, the three of us booked a flight home, accompanied by two nurses. Thank You, Lord, for travel insurance!

I'll never forget that long eight-hour flight. Our travel insurance paid for first-class seats for Ken and his two nurses, and one seat in economy for me. The first-class seats were pods where you could lie down, but due to Ken's long legs he could only partially recline. Every two hours or so I'd leave my seat and check on him. I could tell he was very uncomfortable, judging by the look on his face and the way his eyes searched mine.

By this time, we had worked out a crude way of communicating. He wasn't able to give a thumb's up and couldn't comprehend that a shake of the head meant "no" and a nod meant "yes." But I noticed that he smiled, although a little lopsidedly, when he was pleased with something. So we worked out that if I asked him a question and the answer was "yes," he would give a large smile, and if the answer was "no," he would frown.

Near the end of the flight, I checked on him once more. I bent over to adjust his pillow, and when I told him we only had two hours to go he started to cry. I had thought it would be good news to learn we were almost home, but he was devastated there were still two tortuous hours to go.

An ambulance met us at the airport and brought us directly to Brampton Civic Hospital, where Ken stayed for three months, in rehab once again. Unfortunately, even though Ken worked hard at his exercises, he experienced only slight progress and was disappointed by his minimal improvement.

I dreaded the day when Ken would be discharged from the hospital. He was looking forward to it and counting down the days, but I was afraid that I couldn't handle his care. In the weeks prior to his discharge, the boys and I scrambled to install an elevator where our front steps had been. Our sliding glass door was replaced with an extra wide door that swung open. A friend gave us a hospital bed they weren't using and another friend gave us a used Hoyer lift to assist me in moving Ken. When I learned Ken would be eligible for government-paid homecare, I struggled to hold back tears of relief. My greatest fear was turning into my new reality.

It quickly became evident that I had a choice to make: look after Ken grudgingly, with a poor attitude, or ask God to help me look after Ken in a way that brought Him glory. God was challenging me to serve as He wanted me to. I was an expert at gritting my teeth and doing the right thing even when I didn't want to, but now, with the Lord's help, I needed to do an attitude check and serve graciously and with pure motives.

I asked myself what it meant to glorify God. Is standing in front of thousands of people, preaching an inspiring message, glorifying God? Does writing a song of praise that goes viral glorify Him? Does leading a Bible study or ushering at church on Sunday bring Him glory? All these do, of course, if done with the right motives.

How about encouraging your wife while she battles cancer? How about tirelessly looking after young children, being loyal to an undeserving employer, or submitting to an unreasonable teacher? Do these things bring glory to God? You bet they do!

When God miraculously intervenes in our lives, God is bringing glory to Himself. But when we learn to accept the trials in our lives, learn to live with them and grow spiritually through them, when we are faithful in the little things, then *we* are given the opportunity to bring glory to God.

What if, when we get to heaven, God says, "My child, let Me show you when you glorified My name the most," and turns His spotlight to specific times in our past? What if the spotlight isn't turned to the spectacular events we're proud of and think will be illuminated, but to the mundane tasks when we were faithful and no one was watching? What if He turns the light to a time in my life when I was patiently cutting Ken's food for him? What if submitting to His will by helping Ken with his coat and zipping it up was a time when I brought the most glory to God?

I spent decades praying for and waiting for Ken to be healed, but what if submitting to God's will for my life brought more glory to God than rejoicing over an answered prayer would have? What if, when I get to heaven, I regret not taking advantage of the opportunities to serve in the mundane because I was more interested in serving in the spectacular ways? Jesus, the Son of God, served others. He cooked His disciples fish for breakfast, broke bread, and washed their feet.

Luke 22:27 says, *"For who is greater, the one who is at the table or the one who serves? Is it not the one who is at the table? But I am among you as one who serves."* Oswald Chambers also said it well:

> It is ingrained in us that we have to do exceptional things for God—but we do not. We have to be exceptional in the ordinary things of life, and holy on the ordinary streets, among ordinary people.[9]

Being faithful in the ordinary, mundane moments of life brings glory to Jesus.

———

One of my favourite Old Testament characters is the hero Joseph. His older brothers sold him and then forgot him. His new owner shackled him, took him far away to Egypt, and then sold him as a slave to Potiphar. Over time, Potiphar handed the running of his household over to Joseph. Because Joseph was blessed by God, everything Potiphar owned was blessed also. Then, through no fault of his own, Joseph was wrongly judged and thrown into prison. About two years later, Joseph was miraculously promoted to taking charge of Pharaoh's whole kingdom.

I wonder what Joseph prayed for while he sat shackled in the prison's damp darkness. Did he pray to return home to his father's household where he had been the favourite? Did he pray to be returned to his compliant master, Potiphar? I don't know what he prayed for, but I think I can guarantee he didn't pray to be released into a position of authority in Pharaoh's palace. A slave promoted from prisoner to ruler over a whole kingdom is a master plan only God could dream up.

So why didn't Joseph go straight from Potiphar's house to Pharaoh's palace? Why was the detour to prison needed? I believe that the Lord knew Joseph wasn't ready for the palace yet, that he had to spend time in the prison first. Perhaps Joseph had something more to learn.

---

[9]   Oswald Chambers, *My Utmost for His Highest* (Grand Rapids, MI: Discovery House Publishers, 1992), October 21.

Jesus always knew how to be obedient. He was never disobedient. He never sinned. However, Hebrews 5:8 says, *"Son though he was, he learned obedience from what he suffered."* Jesus learned to be obedient from the hard times. He needed to learn a new, fuller type of obedience. If Jesus, God's son, had to learn this obedience from suffering, then so must we. So did I.

I still struggle to find the perfect balance between praying for miracles and deliverance from trials, and submitting obediently to the furnace that will refine me. Jesus said in Matthew 7:9–11,

> *Which of you, if your son asks for bread, will give him a stone? Or if he asks for a fish, will give him a snake? If you, then, though you are evil, know how to give good gifts to your children, how much more will your Father in heaven give good gifts to those who ask him!*

God is our kind heavenly father who wants only His best for us.

When Jesus was in the Garden of Gethsemane, deep in anguished prayer, He asked to be delivered from crucifixion. It says in Mark 14:36 that he prayed, *"Abba, Father... everything is possible for you. Take this cup from me. Yet not what I will, but what you will."* Jesus asked to be delivered, but then he said "Not what I want, what you want."

We all have trials we wish would go away, difficult pathways the Lord has ordained us to walk down. But the experience shouldn't be squandered. Instead we should learn while traveling through it. If we exhaust all our resources in pleading for mercy and fighting God's will in order to find an easy way out, we may not learn the important lesson of how to submit to Him and how to be obedient to His voice. Hebrews 5:7 says,

> *During the days of Jesus' life on earth, he offered up prayers and petitions with fervent cries and tears to the one who could save him from death, and he was heard because of his reverent submission.*

There's nothing wrong with wanting to be delivered and praying fervently for it. However, we must also submit to God's perfect will for our lives and be obedient to His leading.

There are different types of obedience. One is the act of obeying, or doing what you're told. Your actions coincide with what is asked, but your attitude may not be what it should be. Another type is being willing to obey, or obeying with submissiveness. Before Ken's stroke I obeyed God, but usually grudgingly. After Ken's stroke, God taught me to obey Him with submissiveness.

————

If before Ken's stroke I was having problems coping with Ken's disability and how it affected my life, I was now completely out of my depth and could feel myself slowly sinking and dreading the future. I decided to be willingly obedient, but fear still lurked close by.

God then drew me close and whispered in my ear to trust Him, just like He had twenty years earlier, but this time I sensed that He wanted something more. It felt like I stood on the threshold of a doorway and God was asking me to step through the door, to trust Him at a deeper level than I'd ever done before. The view through the doorway was misty and dim, and I was hesitant to take the next step, not sure exactly what the Lord had in store for me. No definite answer came, just the realization that if I wanted to be obedient to Him I'd have to take this spiritual step of faith by drawing closer and trusting Him completely with my life.

Before Ken's stroke, I had trusted God *in* my life. I'd followed Jesus where He led but kept pointing out the direction I thought He should lead me. This new step of faith meant trusting God at a deeper level *with* my life. God wanted me to pass the controls over to Him, to step out of the shoes of my daily walk and allow Him to step into them. He wanted me to loosen my grip on my own agenda, hopes, and dreams. He wanted me to stop planning how I wanted my life to unfold and submit to what God desired for my life. God wanted me to allow Him to direct the music of my life even if the tune wasn't of my choosing. He wanted me to truly follow where He led.

This was scary. What if God asked me to do something I didn't want to do? What if God led me down a road that looked dark and foreboding? What if, by following this new path, I made decisions that were irreversible if I changed my mind? What if, partway down, I couldn't get back? But that's where faith and trust comes in.

Jill Briscoe, a Christian speaker, editor, and author, once wrote,

> We want God to pour in what we need *before* we start pouring out. We expect Him to pour in some courage before we take action. We expect Him to pour in the strength and inspiration before we obey Him. But it doesn't work that way. We first have to be obedient to the promptings of the spirit—to the ideas He puts in our heads. And then, after obedience, the power comes.[10]

Instead of fighting where I was, I needed to embrace and accept it. Then the Lord would provide what I needed.

So, one sunny day in a park close to our home, I stepped through the arch of an arbour as a symbol of stepping through the doorway God had put before me. Nothing changed immediately, but over the next few days I noticed a freedom and contentment I had never experienced before. It was a mystery. How could I feel freedom when I hadn't been this bound to someone since the boys were babies? Ken's care was constant and required me to stay close at hand. As a result of taking this step of trusting God to a greater degree and putting my life in His hands, He rewarded me with an internal freedom that was brand new. My discontentment dissipated and was replaced with fulfillment. If God wanted my life to be devoted to my husband's care, then I was willing to submit to God's plan.

Now I understood what the apostle Paul meant when he wrote *"offer your bodies as a living sacrifice"* (Romans 12:1) or *"For you died, and* your life is now hidden with Christ in God. *When Christ, who is your* life, *appears, then you also will appear with him in glory"* (Colossians 3:3-4, emphasis added).

---

[10] Jill Briscoe, *A Little Pot of Oil* (Colorado Springs: Multnomah Press, 2003), 64–65.

Jesus said in John 15:13, *"Greater love has no one than this: to lay down one's life for one's friends."*

In *My Utmost for His Highest*, Oswald Chambers wrote,

> For thirty-three years Jesus laid down His life to do the will of His father. "By this we know love, because He laid down His life for us. And we also ought to lay down our lives for the brethren" (1 John 3:16). Yet it is contrary to our human nature to do so. If I am a friend of Jesus, I must deliberately and carefully lay down my life for Him.[11]

Finally! I found the victory I had craved for twenty years. God brought me to the brink of my endurance before I was ready to receive everything He had for me and accept His plan for my life. I hadn't known there was a closer walk than the road I'd been journeying.

Now, each morning, I hand over my day to the Lord. If something unplanned happens, instead of fretting and getting stressed, I step back, put my hands in the air, and let God have control of my day. If everything runs amok, I just wait to see how God will orchestrate events to bring order out of chaos. It isn't my concern, because I've already given the day and my life to Him. Standing back, I let Him deal with it. I just make sure to stay sensitive to His leading and wait for Him to take the next step, freeing me of the heavy responsibility of trying to make everything right.

Over and over in the Gospels, Jesus says, "Follow me." He doesn't stand on the sidelines pointing ahead and telling us to go down the road, turn left at the next crossroad, and then call out after us, "I'll meet you there." No, He just asks us to follow in His footsteps, where He has already been.

The price to walk this path is high. It cost me my agenda for my life. It cost me the right to live my life my way. It cost me my dreams for the future. It cost me myself.

---

[11] Oswald Chambers, *My Utmost for His Highest*, June 16.

But! Yes, there is a big but. The freedom I experience, the joy that bubbles up in me, the cloak of peace that surrounds me with warmth, is well worth the sacrifice of my life. I wouldn't trade where I am now, even with Ken's present disability, with the person I was before his stroke.

Jesus said in Luke 9:23–24,

Whoever wants to be my disciple must deny themselves and take up their cross daily and follow me. For whoever wants to save their life will lose it, but whoever loses their life for me will save it.

I wish I could tell you that all our troubles lifted like early morning mist, but they didn't. Ken is still as severely disabled now as he was a year ago. His right side is still almost completely paralyzed. He can raise his right arm slightly but his hand is unresponsive. His left arm and hand are almost normal, and there is a bit of movement in his right leg, but he is now confined to a motorized wheelchair.

His speech is slowly improving, but he's no longer the chatty individual he once was and struggles considerably to express himself verbally. He is no longer able to drive, nor capable of running his own business, and he even had to relearn how to use a computer. He requires assistance to get in and out of his wheelchair, to dress and eat, and to complete his toileting routine. I sometimes need to interpret to others what he is trying to communicate and still don't know what our future will hold. But I do know this: it isn't my life I'm living. Giving everything to God, I am letting Him orchestrate my life for me.

Oh sure, I have bad days. Days when I find myself struggling to stay afloat and keep my head above the water. I sometimes—or perhaps I should say, quite often—take the reins out of God's hands and try to steer the wagon myself. But God is so patient with me. When I realize what I've done, I just pass the reins back and He gets us on the right trail again. The problem with being a *living* sacrifice is that you keep crawling off the altar.

Are you wondering what area of your life you need to surrender to God? Are you reading this and wondering where your doorway is? If you take your finger and point to your greatest fear, the fear so deep that it's become part of yourself, you're probably pointing to your doorway. Instead of living with this fear, making excuses as to why it's justified and letting it cripple you, hand it over to your Lord. Trust Him.

Why don't you try it? Tomorrow, write your to-do list in pencil and hand the Lord an eraser. Tell Him that He's in charge and you'll follow His lead, even if it means setting aside your own agenda for the day—or facing a fear that scares you. Be prepared to let God be in control. Give your day totally to God, step back, be sensitive to where He leads, and wait for Him to surprise you. You will not be disappointed.

My prayer is that as I follow closely after Jesus, so will you. As He leads, huddle in close behind Him, grasp the back of His cloak, put your feet into His footprints, and let the warmth of His presence enfold you.

If you would like to know more about my book or see family photos, visit www.sharonfaber.com. To contact me, please email sharonrosefaber@gmail.com.